50 Nifty

SPEAKING AND LISTENING ACTIVITIES

Promoting Oral Language and Comprehension

LETRS

Judith Dodson

Cambium LEARNING® Group

Sopris

Printed in the United States of America
Published and Distributed by

4093 Specialty Place • Longmont, Colorado 80504
(303) 651-2829 • www.soprislearning.com

Dedication

This book is all about the magical power of words. I wrote it with the hope that it can help teachers use words like **embraces** to help students feel, when they enter their classrooms, that they are entering a warm and caring circle of words and actions—a place where they are not just shown, but also *told* about their value. Teachers are busy in today's classrooms, and taking the time to simply talk to students sometimes falls prey to the realities of teaching our standards and curriculum and following specific lesson plans. However, talking *is* teaching, and positive and authentic talking can transform a student's experience of school and his concept of himself in ways that are deep and life-changing and sometimes unimaginable to a busy teacher. Teachers have enormous and important positive potential beyond teaching content. This book is meant as a tool to help teachers understand and realize the positive power they have on the lives of their students when they model positive talk and responsive listening in their classrooms, and in so doing teach their students to speak and listen in a positive and engaged manner. It is my hope that this book helps teachers understand that their job is not just to use words to impart information, but to use words to perform magic on a daily basis—to bring learning alive to touch the hearts and minds of their students with the magic and power of words every day.

This book is dedicated to my family for giving me the love and sanctuary of the life we have together. I am blessed by your support, faith, and confidence in me. You are the heart of me and you are at the heart of my work, always.

About the Author

Judi Dodson, M.A., is a national *Language Essentials for Teachers of Reading and Spelling* (LETRS) trainer who works with teachers and administrators of primary, intermediate, and secondary students. She served for 20 years as a special education teacher, primarily with children with reading problems, and as an educational consultant performing diagnostic assessment of learning disabilities. Her first book, *50 Nifty Activities for 5 Components and 3 Tiers of Reading Instruction*, was published by Sopris in 2008.

Judi consults with schools, state departments of education, and school districts on issues related to school change, teacher knowledge, and literacy achievement. She speaks at conferences and gives workshops on topics related to reading intervention and activities that support increasing student achievement. Judi believes that working to empower teachers with knowledge about literacy can make a real difference in their work and help them change and enrich the lives of the children they teach.

Judi lives in the Rocky Mountains of Colorado with her husband and daughter and has two grown sons. She divides her time between her family, writing, teaching teachers, and as president of Peruvian Hearts, a nonprofit organization that supports the education, healthcare, and nutritional needs of children living in orphanages in Peru.

Contents

Foreword

Were you ever in a classroom where the teacher did all of the talking and the students barely said a word? Perhaps that teacher or student was you. It certainly has been me. Yet, research has found in countless ways, many times over, that engagement, practice, and participation characterize classrooms that support student learning. Surely, most of us have heard the saying, "What I do, I remember" — and that is as true for listening and speaking as it is for reading, writing, math, science, or any area of academics we wish to cite. Students must use language purposefully and with guidance to develop effective communication skills.

This anthology of listening and speaking activities is the second in the "50 Nifty" series, following Judi Dodson's first, highly regarded book addressing the five components of reading instruction (*50 Nifty Activities for 5 Components and 3 Tiers of Reading Instruction*). These activities are just as practical, authentic, and adaptable for any classroom. They address fundamental skills such as turn-taking in conversation, active listening, sentence elaboration, and giving compliments. The whole collection targets oral language development at every level, including words, sentences, social discourse, and academic language comprehension and expression. Judi's gentle, loving touch and creative use of simple props give each activity that little extra something that makes it inviting and fun.

Activities will be easy for teachers to inject into classroom routines. It addition, the book provides activities for parents and their children to enjoy outside of school. I suspect teachers will be so eager to use the activities that whole schools will be transformed by Random Words of Kindness, The Conversation Assembly, and the Compliment Box. In short, this book is a wonderful gift to teachers and parents who want their students to listen attentively, engage with one another, and speak effectively. Thank you, Judi, for sharing your splendid teaching ideas.

— Louisa Moats

Introduction

5*0 Nifty Speaking and Listening Activities: Promoting Oral Language and Comprehension* provides teachers with simple, engaging activities to support and enhance oral language development in their students through frequent, distributed practice. The activities have been designed to emphasize active listening, modeling, and frequent opportunities for speaking and responding within the classroom setting. They are connected to vocabulary development, reading, content-area study, and the development of background knowledge within the context of oral-language development. Weak oral language impacts reading comprehension and written language. When teachers work to enhance student instruction in oral language, they will be encouraged by the improvements their students make in both oral and written language. While most teachers are not given the training of speech and language pathologists, focused language activities, such as the ones presented in *50 Nifty Speaking and Listening Activities*, can help classroom teachers reinforce the work of speech and language pathologists and build the oral language skills in those students who have language weaknesses, but are not special education students.

Instructional Practices

The activities in *50 Nifty Speaking and Listening Activities* are designed to help empower all teachers to feel comfortable setting oral language improvement goals for their students. The book is divided into five sections, each representing a language skill area that will be developed: Active Listening, Vocabulary Development, Sentence Building, Learning and Speaking, and Family Connections. **Active Listening** activities emphasize teaching and practicing listening as an active not passive process with the assumption that students only learn when they are listening to us and each other. **Vocabulary Development** activities stimulate vocabulary in engaging ways to increase mastery of the words that have been selected for instruction. **Sentence Building** activities allow students to create and use more elaborate and descriptive sentences so they can better communicate about things that are important to them. **Learning and Speaking** activities provide students with the opportunity to engage in oral discussions as both speakers and listeners. The **Family Connections** section provides ideas for bringing parents in as partners to your oral language goals and activities.

Activity Organization

Each activity is organized similarly, with an activity overview, a link to literacy (that shows how the activity supports literacy development), a family connection activity, and variations for independent and paired practice in addition to whole classroom instruction. Each variation enables students to remain engaged in the learning process. First, students are introduced to a skill in a whole classroom setting; then, students work in small, flexible groupings or they practice the skill on their own with a partner. Each activity allows for a gradual release of responsibility from teacher modeling to guided practice and, ultimately, to independent practice for students.

Sharing the Purpose of the Activity

When students understand how the skills they are learning will help them become better speakers, and eventually, better writers, they are more likely to retain, recall, and apply what they are learning. The activities in this book have been designed to give students enough practice so that they learn to speak and listen with increased skill and confidence. Each activity explains the purpose of the lesson and returns to the purpose later. Sharing the purpose with your students helps them understand why they are doing each activity.

Using a Framework

While there is no general lesson plan in *50 Nifty Speaking and Listening Activities*, the BLISS Strategy provides a five-step framework for approaching oral language instruction with your students. For each activity:

- **B**uild background knowledge about a topic.

- **L**isten actively and speak responsively about the topic.

- **I**ntegrate and connect old knowledge with new learning.

- **S**how your knowledge through discussion, sorting, creating, and writing.

- **S**hare your knowledge about the topic by reading and sharing your work orally.

Linking to Literacy

Learning to speak, unlike learning to read, appears to be a natural process. Students learn to speak by living in an environment that exposes them to words. Students who do not get the exposure to words that others get, are left with a burden for future learning since oral language skills lay down the foundation for literacy development.

The simple view of reading comprehension (Gough & Tunmer, 1986) can be seen as having two main components: decoding and listening comprehension. Listening comprehension depends on a student's background knowledge and oral language skills. When students have deficits in language skills, their ability to read and comprehend is compromised. Teachers' observation of the relationship between thinking and speaking in the classroom happens on a daily basis, and teachers can begin to make a difference by simply, thoughtfully, and intentionally expanding their own language usage in the classroom. This is especially important for students who are not as exposed to rich language usage and exposure at home. In tandem with use of the *50 Nifty Speaking and Listening Activities*, teachers can make a difference when they:

- Use and model verbal reasoning processes in class that may not be modeled orally in the home.

- Develop opportunities for attention and engagement that lead to purposeful listening and remembering.

- Continue to work toward the goal of the expansion and elaboration of vocabulary and syntax as the students' ability to comprehend increasingly complex language increases.

- Increase the intentional and clear use of academic vocabulary within the school day.

- Help students find "talking buddies" (i.e., pairing shy students with more outgoing ones) to increase structured language interaction around words and ideas.

- Ask students to find, point to, label, describe, reflect on, or retell.

- Provide opportunities for direct and indirect language learning, through frequent distributed oral language practice.

- Provide opportunities for building background knowledge throughout the school day.

- ◉ Stimulate meta-linguistic thinking through opportunities for comparing, contrasting, and making reflections on language.

- ◉ Connect opportunities for speaking to opportunities for writing.

- ◉ Check for phonological confusions versus correct perceptions (e.g., shock/shark; conversation/conservation) in students of all grade levels.

- ◉ Label as you teach by identifying things and ideas with words and verbal expansions, providing real context for new words, terms, and concepts (e.g., "A throne is a large and fancy chair that is used by a king").

- ◉ Paraphrase text as needed until deeper comprehension of complex text is possible.

- ◉ Model thinking and speaking as you reflect on reading. This can help students by providing a framework for thinking about the story. The goal is a student-generated reflection on reading.

- ◉ Refine thoughts and grammar with verbal restatement and modeling (e.g., student says, "The boy *runned* quick"; teacher restates, "The boy ran quickly").

- ◉ Include expansion of thoughts by creating a restatement that goes beyond the original sentence and expands it with more detail (e.g., "The boy ran across the playground quickly").

- ◉ Connect new information to old information in a clear and transparent fashion. Help students relate new learning and ideas to background knowledge.

- ◉ Choose vocabulary words thoughtfully (i.e., words that have high utility and can expand critical thinking).

- ◉ Provide opportunities for direct instruction in grammar and sentence structure to support deeper understanding of how to build better sentences.

Family Connections

Children have an early developmental period that is considered by neuroscientists to be a sensitive zone for language development. It is best for that early period to be full of rich language stimulation. Children who do not get the exposure to words that others receive are left with a burden for future learning.

For these reasons, oral language development works best when parents are partners. Even when parents have weak oral language skills themselves, they want what is best for their children. It is our job, then, to help parents understand what they can do at home to support and improve their children's oral language skills. Begin by making them aware of what skills their children should have at each grade level. (See *Table 1.1 Scope and Sequence of Speech and Language Development* on the next three pages.)

Table 1.1. Scope and Sequence of Speech and Language Development

	Kindergarten	First Grade
	By the end of kindergarten your child should be able to do the following:	By the end of first grade your child should be able to do the following:
Listening	• Follow 1–2 simple directions in a sequence • Listen to and understand age-appropriate stories read aloud • Follow a simple conversation	• Remember information • Respond to instructions • Follow 2–3 step directions in a sequence
Speaking	• Be understood by most people • Answer simple "yes/no" questions • Answer open-ended questions (e.g., "What did you have for lunch today?") • Retell a story or talk about an event • Participate appropriately in conversations • Show interest in and start conversations	• Be easily understood • Answer more complex "yes/no" questions • Tell and retell stories and events in a logical order • Express ideas with a variety of complete sentences • Use most parts of speech (grammar) correctly • Ask and respond to "wh" questions (who, what, where, when, why) • Stay on topic and take turns in conversation • Give directions • Start conversations
Reading	• Know how a book works (e.g., read from left to right and top to bottom in English) • Understand that spoken words are made up of sounds • Identify words that rhyme (e.g., *cat* and *hat*) • Compare and match words based on their sounds • Understand that letters represent speech sounds and match sounds to letters • Identify upper- and lowercase letters • Recognize some words by sight • "Read" a few picture books from memory • Imitate reading by talking about pictures in a book	• Create rhyming words • Identify all sounds in short words • Blend separate sounds to form words • Match spoken words with print • Know how a book works (e.g., read from left to right and top to bottom in English) • Identify letters, words, and sentences • Sound out words when reading • Have a sight vocabulary of 100 common words • Read grade-level material fluently • Understand what is read
Writing	• Print own first and last name • Draw a picture that tells a story and label and write about the picture • Write upper- and lowercase letters (may not be clearly written)	• Express ideas through writing • Print clearly • Spell frequently used words correctly • Begin each sentence with capital letters and use ending punctuation • Write a variety of stories, journal entries, or letters/notes

Introduction

	Second Grade	Third Grade
	By the end of second grade your child should be able to do the following:	By the end of third grade your child should be able to do the following:
Listening	↻ Follow 3–4 oral directions in a sequence ↻ Understand direction words (e.g., location, space, and time words) ↻ Correctly answer questions about a grade-level story	↻ Listen attentively in group situations ↻ Understand grade-level material
Speaking	↻ Be easily understood ↻ Answer more complex "yes/no" questions ↻ Ask and answer "wh" questions (e.g., who, what, where, when, why) ↻ Use increasingly complex sentence structures ↻ Clarify and explain words and ideas ↻ Give directions with 3–4 steps ↻ Use oral language to inform, to persuade, and to entertain ↻ Stay on topic, take turns, and use appropriate eye contact during conversation ↻ Open and close conversation appropriately	↻ Speak clearly with an appropriate voice ↻ Ask and respond to questions ↻ Participate in conversations and group discussions ↻ Use subject-related vocabulary ↻ Stay on topic, use appropriate eye contact, and take turns in conversation ↻ Summarize a story accurately ↻ Explain what has been learned
Reading	↻ Have fully mastered phonics/sound awareness ↻ Associate speech sounds, syllables, words, and phrases with their written forms ↻ Recognize many words by sight ↻ Use meaning clues when reading (e.g., pictures, titles/headings, information in the story) ↻ Reread and self-correct when necessary ↻ Locate information to answer questions ↻ Explain key elements of a story (e.g., main idea, main characters, plot) ↻ Use own experience to predict and justify what will happen in grade-level stories ↻ Read, paraphrase/retell a story in a sequence ↻ Read grade-level stories, poetry, or dramatic text silently and aloud with fluency ↻ Read spontaneously ↻ Identify and use spelling patterns in words when reading	↻ Demonstrate full mastery of basic phonics ↻ Use word analysis skills when reading ↻ Use clues from language content and structure to help understand what is read ↻ Predict and justify what will happen next in stories and compare and contrast stories ↻ Ask and answer questions regarding reading material ↻ Use acquired information to learn about new topics ↻ Read grade-level books fluently (fiction and nonfiction) ↻ Reread and correct errors when necessary
Writing	↻ Write legibly ↻ Use a variety of sentence types in writing essays, poetry, or short stories (fiction and nonfiction) ↻ Use basic punctuation and capitalization appropriately ↻ Organize writing to include beginning, middle, and end ↻ Spell frequently used words correctly ↻ Progress from inventive spelling (e.g., spelling by sound) to more accurate spelling	↻ Plan, organize, revise, and edit ↻ Include details in writing ↻ Write stories, letters, simple explanations, and brief reports ↻ Spell simple words correctly, correct most spelling independently, and use a dictionary to correct spelling ↻ Write clearly in cursive

	Fourth Grade	**Fifth Grade**
	By the end of fourth grade your child should be able to do the following:	By the end of fifth grade your child should be able to do the following:
Listening	℮ Listen to and understand information presented by others ℮ Form opinions based on evidence ℮ Listen for specific purposes	℮ Listen and draw conclusions in subject area learning activities
Speaking	℮ Use words appropriately in conversation ℮ Use language effectively for a variety of purposes ℮ Understand some figurative language (e.g., "the forest stretched across") ℮ Participate in group discussions ℮ Give accurate directions to others ℮ Summarize and restate ideas ℮ Organize information for clarity ℮ Use subject area information and vocabulary (e.g., social studies) for learning ℮ Make effective oral presentations	℮ Make planned oral presentations appropriate to the audience ℮ Maintain eye contact and use gestures, facial expressions, and appropriate voice during group presentations ℮ Participate in class discussions across subject areas ℮ Summarize main points ℮ Report about information gathered in group activities
Reading	℮ Read for specific purposes ℮ Read grade-level books fluently ℮ Use previously learned information to understand new material ℮ Follow written directions ℮ Take brief notes ℮ Link information learned to different subjects ℮ Learn meanings of new words through knowledge of word origins, synonyms, and multiple meanings ℮ Use reference materials (e.g., dictionary) ℮ Explain the author's purpose and writing style ℮ Read and understand a variety of types of literature, including fiction, nonfiction, historical fiction, and poetry ℮ Compare and contrast in content areas ℮ Make inferences from texts ℮ Paraphrase content, including the main idea and details	℮ Read grade-level books fluently ℮ Learn meanings of unfamiliar words through knowledge of root words, prefixes, and suffixes ℮ Prioritize information according to the purpose of reading ℮ Read a variety of literary forms ℮ Describe development of character and plot ℮ Describe characteristics of poetry ℮ Analyze author's language and style ℮ Use reference materials to support opinions
Writing	℮ Write effective stories and explanations, including several paragraphs about the same topic ℮ Develop a plan for writing, including a beginning, middle, and end ℮ Organize writing to convey a central idea ℮ Edit final copies for grammar, punctuation, and spelling	℮ Write for a variety of purposes ℮ Use vocabulary effectively ℮ Vary sentence structure ℮ Revise writing for clarity ℮ Edit final copies

Introduction

Then, to help students achieve these goals, convey the information in "Early Elementary Suggestions for Success" or "Later Elementary Suggestions for Success" (below) to parents, depending on the age of their child.

Early Elementary Suggestions for Success	Later Elementary Suggestions for Success
↻ Talk with your child frequently. ↻ Read a variety of books and discuss the stories with your child. ↻ Use rhyming games to help your child focus on sound patterns. ↻ Have your child retell stories and talk about the events of his/her day. ↻ Talk with your child during daily activities (e.g., while making cookies give directions). ↻ Talk about how things are alike and different. ↻ Give your child reasons and opportunities to write.	↻ Continue to encourage reading by finding reading material that is of interest to your child. ↻ Encourage your child to form and express opinions about what he/she hears or reads. ↻ Help your child make connections between what is read and heard in school to what happens at home and in other daily activities. ↻ Talk aloud as you help your child understand and solve problems encountered in reading material. ↻ Help your child recognize spelling patterns (e.g., the beginning of a word, such as *pre-* or the ending of a word, such as *-ment*). ↻ Encourage your child to write letters, keep a diary, or write stories.

Ideas for Partnering with Parents for Oral Language Development

Finally, refer to the following tips for additional ideas about how you and your school community can help create an environment where parents feel needed and involved:

◉ **Encourage reluctant parents with a positive attitude and school climate that encourages parental involvement.** Send out repeated invitations and line your walls with posters and pictures of parents and students.

◉ **Believe in your parents.** Teachers who believe that every parent *would* want to be welcomed into the school as valued members of the community are more likely to get those parents to come in and feel comfortable.

◉ **Know that words matter.** Negative faculty room or office talk matters and can undermine successful efforts for parent involvement. Words reflect thinking and words create thinking.

◉ **Give out random words of kindness.** Call parents often, send notes home on nice note paper, and compliment parents when students do something well.

◉ **Make positive contacts with parents early in the year.** Good news builds a positive climate. If you do not have good news to share, make statements that express positive anticipation of good news.

◉ **Share the talents of students with parents, and reach out to work together to develop those talents.** Say things such as, "I believe that Janie can become a wonderful writer. Will you help me encourage her by being sure she does some extra writing at home?"

◉ **Partner for success by setting specific targeted goals and activities with parents.** Send home an oral language "intervention kit" that contains questions, topics for discussion, pictures for discussion, videos, objects, and books to stimulate oral language at home.

◉ **Create a community of caring.** Schedule parent meetings and offer child care; schedule meetings in the evenings or on Saturdays, and have interpreters present.

◉ **Hold a free classwide or schoolwide book fair.** Ask families or local organizations to contribute books they no longer read or purchased inexpensively. Every family in the school community then gets to "shop" and take home books for free.

Instructional Tips

The following guidelines will help you effectively choose and plan the activities in this book.

1. **Base your instructional choices on assessment results.** Continue to monitor students' progress in order to judge the efficacy of your instruction.

2. **Plan an I Do, We Do, You Do** format, where appropriate. Modeling, guiding practice with feedback, and then releasing the students for independent practice will set the stage for successful learning. Remember that practice does not make perfect; only perfect practice (guided with feedback when necessary) makes perfect.

3. **Create opportunities for frequent, distributed practice**. Frequent, distributed practice is more effective for retention and recall of information than longer, less frequent learning sessions.

4. **Link prior learning to the new learning.** Making these connections for students will increase their understanding and retention of the new information.

5. **Include multisensory aspects of the activities.** The use of multisensory approaches can increase attention, engagement, and retention of information.

6. **Include opportunities for oral language to develop.** Suggestions are embedded throughout the activities that will give students practice in talking, listening, responding, and elaborating on their responses.

7. **Give students opportunities to create their own mental images.** Creating mental images helps deepen the meaning of new words and concepts. It also creates a personal connection to the learning and enhances the retention and retrieval of information.

8. **Incorporate humor into your lessons.** Humor can increase students' attention, motivation, and sense of connection to the learning, which can enhance retention and retrieval of information.

9. **Bundle skills and strategies to maximize opportunities for distributed practice.** Once students have learned a strategy, the strategy can be applied to new learning. For example, when studying a new word, the students can name the sounds and syllables, define the word, and use the word in a sentence.

10. **Modify your instruction if progress monitoring does not show adequate growth.** Progress monitoring is only effective if it drives your instruction. Check regularly for growth in skills and understanding. If you do not see sufficient growth in your students, consider changing the amount of instruction time, the focus of the instruction, and the group size and makeup.

11. **Accelerate as well as remediate.** Let progress monitoring guide your instructional decisions. When learning has been successful, move quickly to the next concept to close the achievement gap.

12. **Connect with your students at their hearts.** Providing eye contact and authentic conversation, as well as linking learning to students' cultural backgrounds and experience, can make the classroom environment more likely to foster engagement and motivation, leading to new learning and greater achievement.

Positive Teacher Talk

Teachers use a lot of language throughout any given school day. Often we are so busy with the content of what we are talking about that we find ourselves less reflective on the quality of our language. Teacher talk makes a difference to students and the classroom climate. The quality of a teacher's language can either encourage students' language usage or lead to more passive communication.

We know the language that students are exposed to at home differs in terms of vocabulary, complexity, and the number of positive statements or affirmations they receive. (Hart & Risley, 1995). Some students have been well prepared for language and literacy instruction. They have been read to, spoken to, and exposed to a wide variety of vocabulary. Other students in your class may have been exposed to a more restricted language, with shorter sentences and fewer vocabulary words.

As teachers, we can level the playing field for all students by being thoughtful and intentional about our own language in the classroom. We can model good language for our students, but just as importantly, our language can entice students into wanting to more fully communicate. Something as simple as asking an open-ended question versus a more closed question that requires a yes or no answer, can make a big difference. For example, you might say to a student, "What do you like to do when you are outside during recess?" instead of "Do you like to play outside during recess?"

Another way teachers can encourage student language usage is through the use of affirmations in the classroom. When students come from homes where fewer affirmations are used, they are very receptive to a teacher who welcomes them into the room and finds positive and encouraging things to say throughout the day. The small gesture of greeting students with a welcome statement, when done consistently, can make them look forward to coming to that teacher's room. Some ideas for welcome statements are: "I am so glad you are here today"; "We missed you yesterday"; or "How did you manage with your homework last night?" (See the activity Random Words of Kindness for additional examples.)

Positive teacher talk can go a long way with families as well. Because of our busy schedules we often find ourselves primarily communicating with parents by phone and for negative reasons. Think about how much you enjoy an appreciative note in your mailbox from the principal. Parents also appreciate that positive recognition about their children. Teacher web pages now offer a good way of communicating with many families, but be careful not to assume that all families will be looking on the Internet for school news. If parents bring students to school, you can relay positive messages face-to-face, but take note of students who ride the bus, walk to school, or carpool. Sending positive notes home, whether by regular mail or e-mail, builds a relationship of positive communication with parents and will always be welcomed. For additional ideas, use activities such as Family Words of Kindness, Family Car Talk Topics, and The Family Compliment Box.

As you use the activities in this book, ask yourself if you are effectively and intentionally using language to draw students toward you and out of themselves. Does your language lead your students to want to engage in more language and communication—sharing and talking about what they are learning, feeling, and doing? Is it getting their attention in a positive way so it can help them to listen? Most importantly, does your language feel positive and good to your students? When a teacher says something positive and encouraging to a student, it is meaningful for him/her on many different levels and can even be life changing.

English Language Learners

The activities in this book can easily be adapted for students who are learning English as a second language. Each activity includes simple suggestions for doing so. The activities can also be modified for use in a second language for those children being taught in their native language.

Oral language development is a critical foundation element for all literacy learning. Weaving oral language opportunities into all literacy learning activities will increase the opportunities for students to practice their newly developing language skills. It takes many opportunities for practice over time for students to develop the skills they need to read, write, and think in their new language.

Here are some general guidelines to help your English language learners (ELLs) succeed:

- Seat students close to where you will be instructing so that they can get more clues for understanding as well as feedback from you. Seating these students near you will help them stay engaged with the lesson, even though their language is limited.

- When appropriate, give the students a preview of the lesson to be taught before presenting it to the whole class.

- Emphasize a multisensory approach to the activities.

- Emphasize oral language development throughout the instructional day for all ELL students in the classroom.

- Read and reread simple texts aloud, in English and in the students' native language when possible, to give students the opportunity to be exposed to good oral language models.

- Use texts that are repetitive and contain rhythmic patterns. Texts should be simple and culturally sensitive. Use clear, short sentences during classroom instruction and discussion, being sure to increase the complexity and sophistication of language as the students' oral language skills develop.

- Accept approximations of words, reinforcing all attempts at oral language. Understand differences of the sounds of the native language and the sounds needed for success in English.

- Give increased "wait time" for children to think about and formulate responses.

Introduction

- Use music and rhythmic activities to enhance oral language engagement and learning.

- Use familiar pictures and objects to enhance oral language practice with the known. Use pictures and objects of new words and concepts to enhance language learning.

- Have students rehearse orally to help them formulate oral language that can then be transferred into writing. Begin writing with structured activities that support the transference of oral sentence formulation to the written form. Support writing with pictures.

- Provide opportunities for modeling, guided feedback, and frequent distributed paired practice to reinforce language learning. Increase the amount of modeling in the I Do, We Do, You Do model.

- Encourage cooperative learning (peer interaction), which increases risk-taking in terms of oral expression because students are part of a group and the group can support their efforts with language.

Section I:

Active Listening Activities

The simple activities in this section are designed to help you create a classroom climate that nurtures and stimulates active listening and oral language development. Students from every background enjoy positive acknowledgment, especially students from homes in which affirmations are not used on a regular basis. All teachers will benefit from improved student appreciation when they provide their students with authentic acknowledgments and affirmations each day. The activities in this section will help encourage everyone in the classroom to communicate more effectively and positively with one another.

Random Words of Kindness

Activity Overview

Students come to school with great differences in the number of affirming statements they experience (Hart & Risley, 1995). The classroom can be a place that begins to level the "affirmation playing field" for students by providing opportunities to develop their listening and speaking skills and providing an environment that nurtures self-esteem and creates a sense of trust and community. Random Words of Kindness is an activity that will help you sincerely express and acknowledge your appreciation for your students. It is not about generating false and inauthentic praise. When students feel that they are part of a nurturing environment they will be more likely to take risks both academically and emotionally.

Materials • • • • • •

- ◎ Self-stick notes
- ◎ Stationery
- ◎ Large picture of a tree
- ◎ Compliment Certificate (see Appendix B)
- ◎ Kindness Chart
- ◎ Heart stickers (for wall chart)
- ◎ Index cards (for wall chart)
- ◎ Kindness Basket (for note paper)

Link to Literacy

Oral language is the foundation for literacy development. Research suggests that students who come from lower socioeconomic households (Hart & Risley, 1995) are often exposed to fewer words and affirmations than other students. This activity increases attention, listening, speaking and writing through the use of affirmations. Increasing skills in these areas can translate to higher levels of motivation, reading comprehension, and writing practice for students in the future.

Whole-Class Activity I

Affirmations

Set the purpose. Say: "We want our class to be a warm and kind place in which to live and learn. We can create that climate by being kind and encouraging to each other. You are always welcome to support others with positive comments throughout the day, but today we're going to do a specific activity where we tell each other things that are positive, friendly, and kind."

1. Begin this activity by creating a "Compliment Circle." Have students sit in a circle. Start by making a positive statement about each student and then have students take turns making positive statements to each other. Make sure no one is left out.

2. In the beginning, there may be some repetition. Accept this as part of the groundwork for students as they develop their own complimenting skills.

3. After your first round of positive statements, have students generate additional ideas of what they could say to each other to be kind, encouraging, appreciative, and positive. Put this list of affirmations on the board or wall, then copy it later for all students to place in a folder or on their individual desks. As an alternative, ask students to choose and write down their five favorite affirmations from the original list.

Return to the purpose. Say: "Thank you for giving your fellow students such wonderful positive comments. Now, practice saying and writing kind messages to your other teachers and family members."

Whole-Class Activity II

Compliment Tree

Before the activity, place a large picture of a tree on a classroom wall. Cut out leaf shapes using self-stick notes so that they can stick easily to the tree.

Set the purpose. Say: "This tree is where we'll make our good feelings grow. Each time I hear positive words spoken by one of you to another student a 'leaf' with those words will go on the tree. We'll also put examples of acts of kindness on the tree."

1. Give students examples of positive words of kindness.

2. Give students examples of acts of kindness.

3. Pick a student who recently performed an act or spoke a word of kindness and have him or her be the first "leaf" on the tree.

Return to the purpose. Say: "_____ (student), thank you for saying (doing) _____ yesterday. Yours is the first leaf of kindness."

Whole-Class Activity III

Kindness Chart

This activity creates a sense of friendly acknowledgment, appreciation, and competition among students for using positive language in the world around them.

Set the purpose. Say: "This chart is a public demonstration of the words or acts of kindness used or done by all of you. When I see or hear about you doing an act of kindness or saying a kind word to someone, I will put a sticker on your name card. We will set an example of kindness for our whole school."

1. Create a large chart in the classroom or the hallway. On the chart, place an index card with each student's name, leaving enough room on the card to place heart stickers for each act or word of kindness. If you post the chart in a more public place (e.g., in the hallway), it will encourage others to give stickers to your students for their kind behavior. It will also encourage and motivate the entire school to participate and will create a more positive school climate. The chart should have two categories: One for home, and one for school, and each category should have a card for each student.

2. Give students an opportunity each day to report any kind word or act they said or performed at home.

3. Place a sticker on a student's name card for each word or act of kindness said or performed at home or at school.

4. Give students examples of words of kindness in various situations: at home, in the classroom, on the playground, at school, and in their communities.

5. Discuss how words of kindness affect others in the world (e.g., writing thank you notes makes others feel appreciated).

Random Words of Kindness

Return to the purpose. Say: "_____ (student), thank you for saying (doing) _____ yesterday. You are a role model for others in our class and at our school."

Independent/Paired Activity I

1. Be a model for encouraging statements. The following are some examples of positive statements you can make to your students throughout the day:

    "I'm so glad you are here today."
    "I can't wait to hear what you think about our story today."
    "What do you think about_____?"
    "You are really working hard on that."
    "Let me know if I can help you with that."
    "It is good to see your smile today."
    "Thank you for sharing with others."
    "Thank you for your kindness."
    "Come and see me for a minute during lunch and we can talk."
    "Come in after lunch for a little treat."

2. After modeling positive comments over time, you can give students a list of examples of positive comments they can make to each other in the future and post the list in the classroom, such as:

    "I'm glad you're here today."
    "Let's play together at recess."
    "If you want, I'll help you during math."
    "Ask if you need help with anything today."
    "Do you want to go to the library together?"
    "Do you want to be reading partners today?"
    "Let's have a snack together today."
    "Let's sit together during lunch today."
    "Let's sit together during circle time today."

Independent/Paired Activity II

1. Keep a "kindness basket" filled with self-stick notes of assorted sizes and colors and inexpensive stationery of appealing colors and designs in the classroom. Tell students that they may pick out a different self-stick note or piece of stationery each day and use it to write a note of appreciation to a friend, teacher, or other person who works at the school.

2. Be a good example of this behavior by writing your own notes of affirmation and appreciation to students regularly. Leave notes on their desks or in mailboxes, or give them to students directly. Make sure each student gets a note every week or two.

Family Connections

1. Have students use the stationery found in the "kindness basket" to write and bring notes home to family members.

2. Send your own positive teacher-to-parent notes to students' families on a regular basis.

3. For additional activities use the Family Words of Kindness and the Family Compliment Box activities in the Family Connections section.

Waves of Words: Classroom Read Aloud

Activity Overview

Waves of Words encourages you to use reading aloud as a tool to build oral language comprehension and expressive skills. Some students come to school having never been read to, and other students have heard hundreds of books before entering kindergarten. This activity offers a chance to help balance these disparate levels of language exposure.

> **Materials** • • • • • • •
>
> ◎ Books of many different genres (fiction, nonfiction, and poetry) and themes

If a teacher reads three books a day to her class, over the course of a school year that amounts to about 600 books. This does not mean that a teacher has to have hundreds of different books to read to her class. At home, a student has many favorite books that a parent reads to him/her over and over again. Similarly, in school a class will have its favorite books and the teacher can read them over and over again to achieve a goal of, say, 1000 books. By choosing books carefully, and including a lot of expository text and poetry, you can build background knowledge and phonological awareness at the same time you expose your students to rich language so they become better prepared to read and comprehend text.

Link to Literacy

Reading comprehension is an amalgam of oral language skills, decoding, vocabulary, and background knowledge. When teachers expose students to a lot of "book language," they enhance their listening comprehension skills, develop their vocabulary, and increase their domain-specific knowledge for greater language comprehension both orally and in text reading.

Whole-Class Activity

Set the purpose. Say: "Every day we are going to take time to read and talk about books. Listening to books being read will help you to become better readers and writers."

Read books to students, trying to vary the subject matter or style as much as possible. Use these ideas:

1. Read new books to students.

2. Read books they have heard before.

3. Read books that relate to a theme of study.

4. Read collections of poetry.

5. Read nonfiction so that you can build domain-specific knowledge at the same time you expose them to great words and language.

Return to the purpose. Say: "You've done wonderfully listening and talking about our books during reading time. Thank you."

Independent/ Paired Activity

1. Give students opportunities to read books independently or with a partner after they have been shared in the large group.

2. Students may create pictures in response to the book.

Family Connections

1. Use the Family Read Aloud Time activity.

2. Use the Fair-Trade Book Fair activity.

3. Send books you've read in class home with students to share with their families.

30-Second Conversation

Activity Overview

The 30-Second Conversation activity engages students in brief, authentic conversations led by the teacher. This quick, one-on-one activity allows teachers to reframe a student's abbreviated, truncated answers into longer responses. In this way, students are exposed to good linguistic models and the kind of authentic conversation that may not take place in their home environments. In addition, this activity gives a student the kind of individual teacher attention that makes him or her feel they are an integral and valued part of the class and school community.

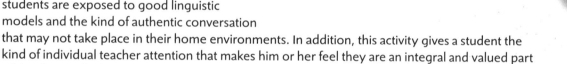

Materials

- Topics of mutual interest between you and each student in the class
- Clock/watch to time sessions

Link to Literacy

Research informs us that children are not always exposed to many words and turn-taking opportunities with language in their home setting (Hart & Risley, 1995). Conversation can be modeled and learned through listening purposefully and responding appropriately. The 30-Second Conversation activity exposes students to good syntax and appropriately challenging vocabulary so that they are better prepared when they encounter complex syntax and vocabulary in their reading.

Independent/Paired Activity

1. Choose those students in your class who appear to have low language skill, are shy, or reluctant to talk.

2. Take 30 seconds each day (or several days a week) to meet with a student for a short, responsive conversation.

3. Make sure the conversation includes some affirmations.

4. Begin and end with appropriate salutations, for example, "Hi, how are you?" "Thanks so much for talking with me today."

5. Set goals for your conversations as they grow and become more natural.

6. Be sure to take turns. Remember that while you want to model good conversational skill, the goal is to slowly release the responsibility for turn-taking and mutual talking to the student, so that the conversation moves from being predominantly teacher-driven to being shared.

7. Allow the students to practice a similar exercise with each other. For example, you might choose to have 30-second conversations between the students as they participate in the

Heroic Conversations activity, or time pairs of students for 30 seconds while they have a conversation based on a topic you assign.

Family Connections

1. Ask students to have a 30-second conversation with family members each night for a week.

2. Ask students to tell about one of their conversations in class.

3. Ask students periodically throughout the school year to share something in class about conversations they have at home with family members.

Buddy Talk

Activity Overview

Buddy Talk enhances purposeful listening and speaking through the use of structured conversations focused on students' personal connections to a targeted word or phrase. Students partner with one another and use the target word or phrase within a meaningful context. This gives students the opportunity to learn new words and immediately place them within a context that connects old learning and background knowledge to new learning. This connection of old knowledge to new enhances the opportunity for learning, retention, and retrieval of the target words. Since Buddy Talk uses partners for oral language practice, it allows both purposeful listening and opportunities for intentional speaking. This is an activity that is useful in many contexts; for example, this activity can help you begin a new unit of study or can be used to introduce figurative language before students encounter it in a story you read to the class.

Materials

- Teacher-selected words or phrases with pictures to enhance meaning
- Teacher-created Talking Buddy list (two buddies per student)
- Student-selected words or phrases
- Passages or stories that contain target words
- Feather boa or other object that can be passed between student partners to enhance engagement, attention, and fun
- Buddy Talk Worksheet (see Appendix A)
- Plastic sheet protectors
- Dry-erase markers
- Self-stick notes

Link to Literacy

The Buddy Talk activity develops a student's ability to make meaningful connections with words or phrases, thereby facilitating retention and retrieval of vocabulary. The words or phrases should be chosen because they have both academic importance and personal utility (are useful on a regular basis) and will reappear frequently in the classroom. These words or phrases will be helpful for students to know and will help deepen their listening, reading, and writing comprehension and expression.

Whole-Class Activity

Create a Talking Buddy list for your classroom. This is a list of partners who you believe will work productively together during oral-language work. Give each student two buddies. Each student may begin talking to one buddy, then move on to share with their second buddy. Take both behavioral considerations and oral-language ability into consideration as you create a Talking Buddy list.

Set the Purpose. Say: "When you make your own connections to words, it will help you to remember them and use them in your own speaking and writing. It will also help you remember what they mean when you encounter them in a story or book you are reading."

1. Introduce a word or phrase that students will encounter in a reading that will follow or that they are currently engaged in, or a word that they will encounter in a new unit of study. For example, a new word = **enormous** (show a picture of mountains) or a new phrase = **a piece of cake** (show a picture of a piece of cake and another picture of someone doing something easily to show its figurative use). Use the idiom in context and ask students which picture they think is the correct one.

2. Question students to generate ideas about the definitions, then directly teach the meanings of the target words and phrases.

3. Give a personal connection of your own. "When I was in Peru, I saw mountains that were enormous." A connection for the phrase might be: "Playing golf is hard for me, but it is a 'piece of cake' for my son, Danny!"

4. Ask each student to get up, walk around the room, and find their first Talking Buddy. You can have this pre-assigned or it can be random.

5. If you are going to use something to pass between each pair of students, like a feather boa, go to each pair and give the first speaker the boa to wear. If you want to emphasize active listening, then you could say to the students, "Today we are going to really pay attention to the importance of listening, so I am giving the boa to the listener. Listening is just as active as talking, so be sure to listen carefully and look at the speaker, make eye contact, and make personal connections in your mind with what the speaker is saying."

6. When you give a signal, have each buddy share a connection with the word or phrase (give them about 1–2 minutes). Have them pass the boa between them when appropriate.

7. Give the class a second signal, and at the signal students can move on to their second Talking Buddy.

8. Have students begin this time by sharing the connection that their first Talking Buddy made as they listened purposefully to him or her (1–2 minutes). This step is crucial because it gives a purpose for listening. This activity teaches purposeful listening in a fun and engaging way.

9. Give a lot of positive reinforcement for the students who remember what their Talking Buddy said previously. Some students may seem like they don't care, but if you give the students who remembered a lot of positive attention (reward them), and talk about how cool it is that one or two particular students did such a good job of remembering, the others will come along eventually and begin really paying attention.

Return to the purpose. Say: "Now you all probably can remember not only your own connection to the word but your buddy's as well! That will help you to remember the meaning when you hear it or encounter it in a story or book you are reading."

Independent/Paired Activity

1. Have students work in pairs to read a story. Give each student a Buddy Talk Worksheet and a written passage in a sheet protector or a book with a story marked to read and a packet of self-stick notes.

2. Either give students a list of Buddy Talk "target" words or ask students to generate a list of Buddy Talk "target" words as they revisit the text.

3. Ask students to write their target words at the top of the Buddy Talk Worksheet.

4. Have students un-
   derline the targeted
   word or phrase if the
   passage is in a plastic
   sheet protector or,
   if it is a larger story,
   have them put a self-
   stick note on each
   page with the target
   words.

5. Have students revisit
   the target words they
   underlined, or put
   self-stick notes by,
   and take turns giving
   a personal connec-
   tion for the words.

6. Have each student
   choose two of the
   words that have been targeted as Buddy Talk words, write them on the Buddy Talk Worksheet, and create a sentence for each word.

Family Connections

1. Explain to students that they can be teachers and teach their family members new words!

2. Have students put their Buddy Talk Worksheets in a plastic sheet protector and take it home.
   Have them ask their family members what connections they can make to the target words
   and phrases.

3. Be sure to discuss the connections with students the next day. Depending on what you think
   is most appropriate for your class, have students write down their family members' thoughts
   or have students discuss the thoughts.

Buddy Talk

The Compliment Box

I'm glad you are here today! ☺

Activity Overview

The Compliment Box encourages affirmations within the classroom setting. Encouraging words give students confidence and courage to take risks and fully engage in the classroom setting. In this activity, students write compliments for other classmates and place them in a teacher-designated box. This box can be added to on a regular basis. The power of this activity comes when the teacher pulls compliments from the box on a regular basis. Students benefit from hearing compliments about themselves repeatedly. They will look forward to compliments being read over and over again.

Materials • • • • • •

- Attractive box
- Pieces of paper on which compliments can be written
- Small wooden tokens (disks of various shapes: hearts, stars, etc., available at most hobby and craft stores)

Link to Literacy

Researchers Betty Hart and Todd Risley (1995) studied the number of positive statements used in the homes of families with varying socioeconomic status. They discovered that parents' authentic affirmations boosted their children's confidence and allowed them to move out of the family setting with more faith in their ability to learn and take risks in school. (This risk-taking and engagement eventually leads to higher levels of achievement and success.)

Homes that used more affirmations also had more extended discussions and the children were exposed to significantly more words. The researchers discovered that higher-income parents had spoken about 500,000 encouragements (about 600 a day) and 80,000 discouragements to their children between the ages of 1 and 3 years, and lower-income parents had encouraged and praised their children approximately 75,000 times and made discouraging statements about 200,000 times. Teachers can make up some of this difference for students by increasing their "positive teacher talk" and developing a climate of affirmations in their classrooms.

Whole-Class Activity

Set the Purpose. Say: "We are going to turn a plain box into a compliment box for our classroom. A compliment is a statement that tells someone what you like about them or what they do that you admire. We will be thinking of positive things to say about our class as a whole and positive things to say about each member of our class."

1. Give the students note paper, or wooden discs, and pens with which to write compliments for other students and the teacher. (If you are using wooden tokens and the surface area is

small, have students write their compliments on paper first, then neatly rewrite them on the token.)

2. Sometimes give students the opportunity to read their compliments out loud after they write them and then put them in the box.

3. Take time each week to read the compliments that are in the box to the class.

4. **Affirmation Celebration:** Develop a way of keeping track of the number of compliment notes that are written in your classroom. This can be done with a "rock jar"—a stone (or jelly bean) can be placed in a small jar every time a student puts a compliment in the Compliment Box. When the jar is full, the class has an Affirmation Celebration. This can take the form of a popcorn party, extra recess, etc. Be sure to use a small jar that can be filled easily so the celebrations come regularly, reinforcing the positive student behavior of sharing compliments with each other.

5. **Graphing Affirmations:** Put up a "compliment graph" in your classroom. One column on the graph should be for whole class compliments, one for compliments about behavior during recess (or whatever other behavioral goal you are working on), and one for general individual compliments. Your class will see their compliments grow and will want to continue the behaviors that are complimented in addition to the behavior of giving compliments.

Return to the Purpose. Say: "Learning to give compliments to each other is going to make us all feel good about ourselves and each other, and will make our class a warm and caring place to be."

Family Connections

1. Use The Family Compliment Box activity.

The Compliment Box

The Storyteller's Circle

Activity Overview

It is important to create opportunities in the classroom where students can speak and listen in an engaged manner. The Storyteller's Circle activity encourages students to speak in front of a group in order to feel the power of oral language when they receive positive attention from listeners. Having the student tell riddles, jokes, and funny stories is often a good way to get started with this activity, since making the rest of the class laugh gives a lot of positive feedback to the student who is speaking.

Materials • • • • • • •

- Microphone (this could be plastic)
- Story prompts
- Riddle and joke books
- Becoming a Good Listener, Speaker, and Writer (see Worksheet 2 in Appendix A)

This activity can be done in an open-ended manner in terms of topic or you can assign topics; for example, one week the topic can be jokes or riddles, another week funny stories, another week pet or animal stories, another time stories of kindness, etc. While this activity goes a long way toward building a positive climate for oral language in the classroom, it is still important to set norms around listening respectfully (see Becoming a Good Listener and Becoming a Good Speaker sections of Worksheet 2 in Appendix A). All students will understand the importance of these standards of behavior after you remind them that they will also be the storyteller some day, and they'll want others to be respectful of them. Try this activity and you'll notice that even your shy students want to be the storyteller because of how much this activity is enjoyed by the entire class.

Link to Literacy

The Storyteller's Circle supports literacy development by enhancing a student's abilities to use language and listen to language in an engaged and active manner. The more deeply a student understands that all language comprehension is engaged and active, the better he or she will be able to comprehend at both the oral and written level.

Worksheet 2

Becoming a Good Listener, Speaker, and Writer

I. Becoming a Good Listener:
I will look at the speaker.
I will remain just as active when I listen as I am when I am speaking.
I will not interrupt until the speaker is done with his or her turn.
I may nod my head to show that I am following along.
I may ask questions that relate to what the speaker has said when there is a pause in speaking.
I may share my own connection with what the speaker has just said.

II. Becoming a Good Speaker:
I will look at the listener.
I will check to see if the listener understands me:
  ○ Is he or she looking at me?
  ○ Is he or she nodding?
  ○ Does he or she look confused?
I can ask questions of the listener to check if he or she understands me, such as:
  ○ Is that clear?
  ○ Do you follow me?
  ○ Do you have any questions?
I may use gestures to clarify what I want to communicate.
I may change my voice to help express and clarify what I want to communicate.
I will plan time for the listener to be able to respond to what I have said.

III. Becoming a Good Writer:
I will remember that the words I think about and say are connected to the words I will write down.
I will think about what I want to write in my head.
I will picture what I write as I think about it.
I will talk about what I am going to write to my teacher or classmate.
I will draw pictures, make a story map, or fill in a graphic organizer before I start to write.
I will share my writing aloud with my classmates, then add or change my writing if needed.
I will make a final copy of my writing with any changes to make it just right!

Whole-Class Activity

Set the Purpose. Say: "This activity will make you more comfortable speaking and listening to your classmates. Listening to stories will also help you to understand stories when you read. Let's have fun listening and speaking to each other!"

1. Talk to your class about creating class norms for listening. Discuss the fact that listening is active just like speaking. Use Section I ("Becoming a Good Listener") of the Becoming a Good Listener, Speaker, and Writer worksheet to help you set norms that will create a climate of kindness in your classroom.

2. Talk to the class about the role of the storyteller. Review how to become a good speaker. Use Section II ("Becoming a Good Speaker") of the Becoming a Good Listener, Speaker, and Writer worksheet.

3. Model storytelling by telling a story yourself and letting your class practice their active listening skills. Be sure to set a time limit, and tell the class that no story can be more than 2–3 minutes long.

4. Allow the class to respond to your story with questions and comments (set a time limit for this as well).

5. Put up a poster that lists some topics for storytelling. You can create this poster yourself, or you can have your class generate topics (e.g., a funny story, a story from history, joke of the day, an embarrassing moment, an animal story, a family story, or a hero story) to list on the poster.

6. Choose a student to tell a story, using his or her own topic or one from the poster list, and repeat this activity.

7. Scaffold for more reserved or low-language students:

    ◔ Give students a riddle book or "knock-knock" joke book and have them take it home and practice telling a riddle or joke.

    ◔ Let students practice with you before presenting to the class.

    ◔ By giving the student something funny to present, you are assuring that he or she will have the good feeling of making the class laugh, will be seen in a positive light, and then will associate speaking with positive feelings.

Return to the Purpose. Say: "It is fun to speak and listen to each other. Speaking and listening will also help us understand what we read and will help us to be better writers as well."

The Storyteller's Circle

Independent/Paired Activity

1. Have each student work with a partner.

2. Have students go to their seats and draw a picture of an important image they made in their minds while they were listening to one of their classmates.

3. Ask students to take turns either orally retelling a portion of the story or the whole story to each other. If the student with stronger oral language goes first, the weaker language student can use the stronger student's first retell to support his or her retelling.

4. Let partners know that they can help each other by prompting when one person forgets something.

5. Students who are capable can write a summary of the story.

Family Connections

1. Have students practice jokes, riddles, and stories at home with family members.

2. Encourage students to ask family members for ideas about family stories, jokes, or riddles that they might know.

Speaking From the Heart

Activity Overview

Speaking From the Heart emphasizes the idea that both the listener and speaker have an active role to play in conversation and communication. During a conversation, a symbolic heart is passed back and forth between two students. This activity is similar to the Buddy Talk activity in that it enhances purposeful listening and talking in addition to structuring conversations around a student's personal connection to a targeted concept that is part of a unit of study. It is useful in many contexts; for example, it can be used at the beginning of a new unit of study or while introducing new figurative language.

Materials

- A heart-shaped object (e.g., an index card with a heart sticker, a stuffed heart, a heart-shaped pebble, or a heart-shaped slinky) to be passed between speakers
- Teacher- or student-selected concepts with pictures to enhance meaning
- Age-appropriate passages for students to read
- Index cards

Link to Literacy

Speaking From the Heart develops a student's ability to make meaningful connections with new concepts, thereby facilitating retention and retrieval of vocabulary and content. The concepts should be chosen because they have both academic importance and personal utility and are part of a unit of study in the classroom.

Whole-Class Activity

Set the purpose. Say: "When we talk about ideas we are learning about, we become better speakers and listeners and we get better at understanding what we hear and read. Learning to communicate well is fun and enjoyable and helps us become better friends to each other."

1. Introduce a concept that students will encounter in a reading or in a unit of study that will follow or that they are currently engaged in. Eventually students may choose their own topics to discuss.

2. Give a personal connection of your own: "When I **collaborate** with a friend, we help each other and get more done." A connection for one of the phrases might be: "I was glad you helped me clean my room because **I bit off more than I could chew** in the short amount of time I had to clean it, and our collaboration helped me get it done."

3. Ask each student to get up, walk around the room, and find their Talking Buddy or Heart Partner. You can have this pre-assigned or it can be random. When students encounter their partners, give one student in each group the "heart" that they will share. (The speaker may

start with the heart or you may decide that you want to emphasize the listener in this activity and they may hold the heart.) The "heart" can be any of those suggested in the Materials section, or you can have students create their own stuffed heart as a class (cutting out the material, stuffing, sewing, and decorating it) prior to this activity. You could give the other partner a heart slinky. Having something

to do with her hands can help a student focus and remember that listening is as active as speaking.

4. Have the first speaker in each pair share a connection with the concept chosen (give them about 1–2 minutes). Then, ask the listener to pass the heart to the second speaker as he or she gets ready to share.

5. Ask a few students to share aloud what their Heart Partner shared with them about the concept.

6. Give a lot of positive reinforcement for the students who remember what their Heart Partner said previously. Some students may seem like they don't care, but if you give the students who remembered a lot of positive attention (reward them), and talk about how cool it is that they did such a good job of remembering, the others will come along eventually and begin really paying attention.

Return to the Purpose. Say: "Now you all can remember not only your own connection to the topic but your Heart Partners' connection as well! This will help deepen your understanding of the topic when you hear it or encounter it in a book you are reading or as part of a discussion."

Independent/Paired Activity

1. Give each pair of Heart Partners a reading passage that is at an appropriate level for them. It is best if it relates to a topic you have been discussing in class.

2. Give each partner two index cards (each pair gets four cards total).

3. Have Heart Partners work together to read their passage. In this activity, the "heart" first goes to the reader as he or she reads a sentence (lower-reading level) or a paragraph (higher-reading level). The listener follows along.

4. Then, the first reader becomes the listener and gives his or her partner the heart to hold on to while reading the next section. The pairs continue back and forth until the passage is completed. This passing of the heart gives students confidence, makes the reader's role something special, and helps focus listener attention on the reader.

5. When the Heart Partners are done reading their passage, have them work together to choose four new or interesting words that were in the passage and relate to the original topic. For example, if the topic is **collaboration**, words connecting to that might be **help**, **assist**, **cooperate**, and **working together**.

6. Using their index cards, have each partner neatly write one word on each index card.

7. When they have their four words, ask them to exchange their cards with another pair of Heart Partners. Then, have them tell each other a personal connection to these new words. Ask them to "speak from the heart."

Family Connections

1. Have students write notes to family members that use their Speaking From the Heart activity words of the day. For example, if the words were **collaborate** and **responsible**, they could write:

   Dear Mom,
   I want to be more **responsible** about helping with our puppy Rosie. I promise to **collaborate** with you on ways I can help.

2. Have students take the notes home and give a special reward to those students who bring their notes back with a parent signature.

Speaking From the Heart

Growing Words Wall Chart

Speaking Ladder

Activity Overview

The Growing Words Wall Chart helps students monitor their own oral language development. This activity involves the creation of a wall chart that will show the growth of your students' oral language development in terms of active listening, classroom participation at the oral level, and speaking and writing. Be sure to place the chart next to a copy of the Becoming a Good Listener, Speaker, and Writer worksheet (see Appendix A) so that students will learn how to become good listeners and speakers. Adjust the worksheet for your students' age level.

Link to Literacy

Increasing oral language skills can enhance reading comprehension. Charting students' individual growth in those critical skills encourages and motivates them to continue to improve their skills.

Materials • • • • • • •

- ◉ The Ladder Template (see Appendix B) can be mounted on a bulletin board
- ◉ The Clothesline Template (see Appendix B) can be mounted on a bulletin board
- ◉ Becoming a Good Listener, Speaker, and Writer (see Worksheet 2 in Appendix A)
- ◉ Index cards cut out into pants, shirt, dress, or skirt shapes
- ◉ Assorted stickers or small pictures of each student in your class

Whole-Class Activity

Growing Words Wall Chart—Ladder Motif

Set the purpose. Say: "Good speaking, listening, and writing is hard work. Each week there are different goals to help you become better speakers, listeners, and writers. The Ladder will help us watch your skills grow. Each time I see you give a good example of speaking, listening, or writing, you'll move higher up the ladder until you reach the top of the chart!"

1. Use one Ladder Template per student.

2. The first time you see a good example of a student speaking, listening, or writing (making use of the goals you have taught in each of those categories), put a sticker or the student's picture on the first rung of the ladder. Sample goals for this Growing Words Wall Chart can be found on the Becoming a Good Listener,

Worksheet 2

Becoming a Good Listener, Speaker, and Writer

I. Becoming a Good Listener:
I will look at the speaker.
I will remain just as active when I listen as I am when I am speaking.
I will not interrupt until the speaker is done with his or her turn.
I may nod my head to show that I am following along.
I may ask questions that relate to what the speaker has said when there is a pause in speaking.
I may share my own connection with what the speaker has just said.

II. Becoming a Good Speaker:
I will look at the listener.
I will check to see if the listener understands me:
  ◦ Is he or she looking at me?
  ◦ Is he or she nodding?
  ◦ Does he or she look confused?
I can ask questions of the listener to check if he or she understands me, such as:
  ◦ Is that clear?
  ◦ Do you follow me?
  ◦ Do you have any questions?
I may use gestures to clarify what I want to communicate.
I may change my voice to help express and clarify what I want to communicate.
I will plan time for the listener to be able to respond to what I have said.

III. Becoming a Good Writer:
I will remember that the words I think about and say are connected to the words I will write down.
I will think about what I want to write in my head.
I will picture what I write as I think about it.
I will talk about what I am going to write to my teacher or classmate.
I will draw pictures, make a story map, or fill in a graphic organizer before I start to write.
I will share my writing aloud with my classmates, then add or change my writing if needed.
I will make a final copy of my writing with any changes to make it just right!

Speaker, and Writer worksheet (see Appendix A). The language on this worksheet can be simplified or expanded depending on the grade and ability level of the students.

3. Each subsequent time a student is acknowledged by you for doing a good job speaking, listening, or writing, he or she gets to move the sticker or picture up a rung. When a student is on the top rung of the ladder, he or she gets a predetermined reward.

4. When a student gets to the top of all three ladders, give him or her a really special reward.

5. The goal of the activity is that by the time students have reached the top of all three ladders, their good listening, speaking, and writing behaviors have become habits.

6. Model this activity once, using a student who was a good listener that day (e.g., "John, thank you for paying attention during our Buddy Talk activity. I'm going to put this giraffe sticker on the first rung of your ladder.").

Return to the purpose. Say: "We are going to watch our charts as we all become better speakers, listeners, and writers."

Growing Words Wall Chart — Clothesline Motif

1. Use one Clothesline Template per student.

2. Each time you see a good example of a student speaking, listening, or writing (making use of the goals you have taught in each of those categories), place an article of index card "clothing" on the student's clothesline. Sample goals you can teach for this Growing Words Wall Chart can be found on the Becoming a Good Listener, Speaker, and Writer worksheet (see Appendix A). The language on this worksheet can be simplified or expanded depending on the grade and ability level of the students.

3. When a student gets a predetermined amount of clothing on the line, he or she gets a reward.

4. When all three of a student's clotheslines are full, give him or her a really special reward.

5. Model this activity once, using a student who was a good listener that day (e.g., "John, thank you for paying attention during our Buddy Talk activity. I'm going to put a shirt on your clothesline.").

Growing Words Wall Chart

Puppet Play

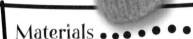

Activity Overview

Puppet Play is not a specific activity but rather contains ideas for the creation and use of puppets to enhance oral language in your classroom. Puppet Play motivates students to become excited about opportunities to practice their oral language skills. Puppets encourage students' attention and listening. Using them takes advantage of the tendency for students to open up more verbally (expressing thoughts and emotions) when they engage in puppet play. For example, when introducing phonemic awareness concepts, interaction with puppets can help heighten students' awareness of the sounds that are practiced because they are "talking" with, and through, the puppets. This is especially true for English language learners.

In the Puppet Play activity, ideas are given about how to use puppets to complement classroom activities such as storytelling, introducing new vocabulary, and reinforcing recent reading. Puppets can help create a greater impact when new vocabulary words and concepts are introduced. And, puppets encourage students' risk-taking in terms of language usage and pronunciation. Additionally, when young students use a puppet, they are often more comfortable and, therefore, more effective in their ability to recall and share newly learned information.

Materials • • • • • • •

- Finger puppets and hand puppets
- Materials for making puppets (paper bags, socks, tongue depressors, buttons, markers, and felt)

Link to Literacy

Enhancing oral comprehension and listening is related to enhancing reading comprehension. Puppet Play can be used to focus listening and a more thorough retelling of recently read and studied text.

Whole-Class Activity

Puppet-Making Ideas

Students will be even more motivated to use puppets within the classroom setting if they make them themselves. The intention of this arts and crafts project is not the creation of the puppet, but rather, to encourage the continued use of the puppet within the classroom, and support oral language practice. Have students make puppets out of a combination of paper bags, socks, inexpensive gloves, and tongue depressors.

Some good Web sites to give you additional puppet-making ideas are: http://familycrafts.about.com/od/puppets/Puppet_Craft_Projects.html and http://www.teacherhelp.org/puppets.html.

Active Listening Activities

Set the purpose. Say: "Puppets are fun to listen to and to make talk. We are going to use puppets in a variety of ways as we speak, learn new words, read, and talk about what we have been reading."

1. Introduce a special puppet that you have chosen to become a part of your classroom. Pass the puppet around, letting students touch it and try it out. This can be done in a large group or during a small group time. You can introduce the puppet to small groups for a few minutes in a small group setting.

2. Keep a basket of small finger puppets and hand puppets that students can choose from to use in various activities. Over time, students will choose their favorite puppets. These "favorites" will help to encourage risk-taking with language usage activities.

3. Follow some basic guidelines when using puppets. Use puppets when encouraging social interaction and discourse among students (and students and teachers) to facilitate work in a large group (with either you using the puppet to talk to the class or a student using the puppet to talk to the class). Use puppets when students are working in pairs asking questions about reading or theme concepts, interviewing, retelling, using vocabulary, etc. Use puppets when storytelling, as related to social and academic learning, introducing new vocabulary, and introducing and reinforcing social studies concepts (e.g., two "puppet-colonists" talk about surviving in the early American colonies, one "Union-puppet" and one "Confederate-puppet" debate the causes of the Civil War, or "puppet-citizens" explain the

values of the Roman Empire). Have students use puppets when they respond to literature or retell stories, during phonemic awareness practice, and when students "touch and say" sounds in one-syllable words or touch the syllables in multisyllabic words. Puppets can also be given to second-language learners to encourage them to speak more in English by letting them "speak" through the puppet.

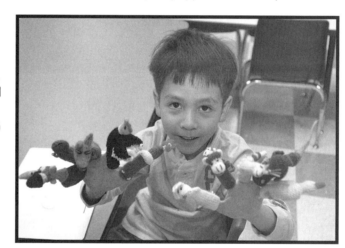

4. Follow these teaching tips when using puppets:
   - Make eye contact between your puppet and the students.
   - Remember that students will pay the most attention to the puppet, not your mouth, so don't worry about not appearing to be a ventriloquist.
   - Modulate your voice for emphasis (e.g., when your puppet whispers, students will listen closely).
   - Develop a character for your puppet so that students will feel that they understand the puppet's personality. This will allow you to use your puppet for solving social problems in the classroom.

Return to the purpose. Say: "Using our puppets makes talking and listening even more fun!"

Independent/Paired Activity

Working in pairs with their puppets, have students ask and respond to questions about reading and content-area concepts, interview each other, or talk about vocabulary.

Vocabulary Development Activities

Teachers observe the relationship between thinking and speaking in the classroom on a daily basis. Speaking both reflects a person's thinking and furthers his thinking. When you give students new words and concepts to think about, you facilitate their ability to engage in more effective critical thinking. Understanding the reciprocity between thought and the expression of thought in spoken language is critical for creating instruction that enhances vocabulary and language skills.

The activities in this section are designed to actively engage students in vocabulary instruction and application. Students will use words in purposeful activities that help them to share and apply their new knowledge. By doing these activities, students will have a better chance at remembering important words and retrieving them for application. They will learn to think about words flexibly and expand their semantic maps of words they already know. While growing vocabulary is important, it is most effective when the words are used and shared in meaningful situations.

Vocabulary Connections

Activity Overview

Vocabulary Connections encourages students to look at words that are closely related but still different and to think of concepts that exist beyond the target words, thereby expanding their semantic maps for those words. For example, if students are given the word **chair**, the goal would be to help them think about definitions of **chair** that go beyond the chair at their desks or dining room table. A chair can be a tree stump around a campfire, a folding beach chair, a swing in a tree, or a throne for a king. Stretching the mental model of a chair allows students to think more expansively and more critically about something so simple. If students are studying different cultures, they can also begin to think about what a chair means for that culture. This further expands their understanding of the world.

The Vocabulary Connections activity helps students build background knowledge about targeted words, think about words and their relationship to each other, and then create a Vocabulary Connections book of their own that showcases their illustrations, sentences, and knowledge of related words.

(**Note:** This activity was inspired by the work of authors Judy Mullen-Schneider and Mary Konrad-Weeks in *But Not Quite!* [2004], which is included with the optional manipulatives kit. Their book shows pictures of items that are similar yet different, such as a mitten that opens and is transformed into a glove. Around the edge of the page are also small pictures of other kinds of gloves and mittens, such as an oven mitt, a catcher's mitt, a gardening glove, and a work glove.)

Materials

- *But Not Quite!* (see Resource section)
- Vocabulary Connections Word List (see Appendix B)
- Pictures and objects for many of the words in the Vocabulary Connections Word List
- Paints, markers, pens, and pencils
- Glue and tape

Link to Literacy

Metalinguistic thinking refers to one's ability to think about and compare and contrast language concepts. This activity gives direct practice as students compare and contrast words and work to understand the context in which they occur in the world. This activity has an impact on students' ability to think about concepts that they encounter during listening and

reading. It is excellent for English language learners and English speakers who have weak vocabulary and oral language skills.

Whole-Class Activity

Set the Purpose. Say: "We are going to think and talk about how we can compare words to each other. We will think about words that are similar, but still somewhat different. For example, a mitten and a glove are similar yet different! Understanding how words are related and how they vary from one another will help you have more background knowledge to apply to your reading and listening."

1. Choose target words for discussion (if you have the book *But Not Quite!* you can use that as a starting point).

2. Discuss the target words with students and generate ideas about other words that are related to the target words. Have pictures or objects representing the target words to make sure that all students have a mental model of them. Have pictures available for as many of the related words generated as possible.

   Have students stand in front of the classroom holding either the pictures or objects and sort themselves according to category (i.e., mittens on one side and gloves on the other). Generate ideas, background knowledge, and discussion based on the classroom sorting activity.

3. Create one or two posters for the target words and the related words. Include all the pictures of words generated. Some ideas for target and related words are:
   - **house** and **tent** (use pictures of a small house, mud hut, igloo, and mansion)
   - **cup** and **glass** (use pictures of a coffee cup, mug, measuring cup, wine glass, stein, and sippy cup)
   - **chair** and **sofa** (use pictures of a porch swing, infant car seat, sleeper sofa, school desk with chair, and church pew)
   - **shoe** and **boot** (use pictures of a fireman's boot, high-heeled shoe, evening slipper, ballet slipper, tap shoe, and fur-lined snow boot)

4. Have the students work with a carefully chosen partner or a small group to create a page for a class-made Vocabulary Connections book. (The book *But Not Quite!* will be an invaluable resource for students as they create their books.) Students can decide which words they want to include in their book (have them choose two words per page) and divide up the pages between themselves. Leave time for discussion in the small groups, so students can thoughtfully decide on their target and related words and how they will create pictures for both.

5. Let students draw their pictures or, if your school has Internet access, allow students to find and print pictures that match their words.

6. Have students write sentences that show their understanding of the meaning and context of the two words on each page of their book.

7. Have materials available for book-making and help students bind their individual sheets together to make a book.

8. Give students in your class an opportunity to share the pages they have created with each other, reading and explaining the connections between the target words and the related words.

9. Arrange for students in your class to share their book with younger students, reading to their classes and explaining the connections between words.

Vocabulary Connections

10. Keep each book your class creates in your classroom library.

Return to the purpose. Say: "By comparing and contrasting the words you chose, you have deepened your understanding of your original words and learned many new words as well."

Family Connections

1. Students may create 1 or 2 pages of their Vocabulary Connections book as a home project.

2. Encourage students to ask family members if they can think of any other examples of words that are related to the target words students have chosen.

Select and Connect

Activity Overview

In the Select and Connect activity, students collect names, words, or phrases that are related to a topic of study, story, book, or film. Students are given a list and asked to connect any two words on the list based on knowledge they have about the topic. (Select and Connect can be done with pictures as well, to augment and develop the students' mental model.) This activity can be used before, during, or after reading or teaching a unit of study. At the beginning of a unit or story, it is a good assessment of students' prior knowledge. During reading or study, the activity can help students make additional connections as they develop more knowledge of the subject. After reading, it can be used as an informal assessment of students' acquired knowledge. Select and Connect is especially effective when students add to each other's linguistic processing by working together to compare and collaborate on responses.

Materials

- Index cards
- Pictures
- Yarn
- Magnetic tape
- White board
- Lists of essential words (from current reading text or related to currently taught topics)
- Select and Connect Worksheet (see Appendix A)

Link to Literacy

Making connections between two ideas and concepts is good practice for making connections during reading. By flexibly matching words with words and pictures with words, students are activating and adding to their background knowledge and deepening their mental model of these words. These models can later be used to enhance comprehension in other situations.

Whole-Class Activity

Set the purpose. Say: "We are going to be figuring out how two things go together. When I say peanut butter what do you think of? Jelly, bread, sandwiches, and cookies? Those are all good connections. There isn't just one right answer. There are many good ideas that you may think of, depending on what your experience with peanut butter has been. We are going to be connecting things we are reading and things we are learning in the same way as we just connected peanut butter and jelly!"

This activity can be used in three stages: Before Reading or Study, During Reading or Study, and After Reading or Study.

Select and Connect

Before Reading or Study

Prepare some pictures and words that are related to a story or unit of study you are working on. Place these "Select and Connect" words on index cards. Put magnetic tape on the back of the index cards so that you can put them up on a white board at the front of the class.

1. Put the pictures and words in two separate columns on the white board.

2. Model one connection by drawing a line between the two index cards to show their connection. Use the word(s) chosen in a sentence.

3. Ask students to select two words or pictures on the board. Ask them to state one connection to the class.

4. Then, have students turn to their neighbors and share another connection.

5. Call on three students to come to the board, "select and connect," and then make sentences that explain their connections.

This can be done successfully before or after reading. After reading, it can be seen as an informal "post-assessment."

Note: Another approach is to give the pictures and words to students and have them line up in two lines. When they make their selection and connection, the two students who are connecting can come into the middle of the two lines (almost like a line dance in square dancing). They can hook arms, put their cards together etc., as they make their connection by creating good sentences that demonstrate how their cards connect.

During Reading or Study

Return to this activity throughout your unit of study, or while you are finishing a story, and ask if any student can now make new and different connections with the pictures or words.

After Reading or Study

Use the activity as an informal learning assessment.

Return to the purpose. Say: "When you can make connections and explain them to others, it shows that you are thinking deeply about what you are learning."

1. Have students work with a partner.

2. Give students index cards and yarn. Have them copy the "Before Reading or Study" words (one per card) on the index cards. Let them also add other words they have learned about that relate to the topic.

3. Working on the floor or at a table with their partners, ask students to make connections by placing yarn between the index cards.

4. The final step is to have students copy these "Select and Connect" words onto their Select and Connect Worksheets. Instead of yarn, have them draw lines between the connected words. Then, ask them to choose their three favorite connections and write them at the bottom of the worksheet.

Family Connections

Use the Family Select and Connect activity for a family-focused version of this activity.

Painting Pictures Together

Activity Overview

Painting Pictures Together is an activity that engages students as active listeners as they work to build a group image (collaborating with other students) that can describe a particular high-utility vocabulary word. Making mental pictures is a foundational comprehension strategy that's critical for deeper understanding of text. Good readers make pictures in their minds as they read. Good listeners make pictures as they listen. These pictures can then be used as a reference for comprehension and recall. Thinking flexibly with words deepens understanding and is a valuable skill in terms of oral and written expression.

Materials

- Words and topics to help students create mental images
- Drawing paper
- Writing paper
- Painting Pictures Together Worksheet (see Appendix A)
- Hand clappers
- Koosh ball

Link to Literacy

When students describe the image they associate with particular text or oral information, they lay the groundwork for being able to reference this image for later writing and speaking.

Whole-Class Activity

Set the Purpose. Say: "Good readers make pictures in their minds when they read. This activity will help you use mental pictures to better understand and retell stories both aloud and in writing."

1. If you have space, have students sit in a circle for this activity. Remind them that good listeners stay focused and active as they listen.

2. Begin with an idea that is motivating and highly visual, such as a clown, a tree house, or a robot.

3. Model a beginning image for the students. **Say:** "I am thinking of a clown with red hair." Ask all of the students to think about this clown.

4. **Say:** "Pass," and ask the student to your right to add to or change the image. You might throw a Koosh ball to another student instead of going in order, because this tends to keep attention more focused. That student may say, "I am picturing a clown with red hair and a big red nose." Ask all students to change the image in their minds from the previous image to the one described by the student.

5. Continue around the circle with students changing their mental images as each student contributes. For example, if one student says, "I am picturing a clown with green hair and a big red nose," then all the children need to change their mental image of the clown's hair.

6. Continue this process until all students have contributed.

7. Distribute plastic hand clappers to the students.

8. Draw the final clown that was described on the front board, one detail at a time, orally repeating the description as you draw.

9. Students can use their plastic hand clappers to show their agreement with each detail that you put in your drawing. This process of comparison and approval with their own individual mental pictures deepens their image and memory.

10. Let students remind you to fill in details that you might intentionally leave out. This will encourage their attention and participation.

Return to the purpose. Say: "You have just practiced making pictures in your mind. That is what good readers do when they read. Making pictures in your mind will help you understand what you listen to and read. This activity will help you use mental pictures to understand and retell stories aloud and in writing."

Independent/Paired Activity

1. Have students work with partners.

2. Give each pair of students two copies of the Painting Pictures Together Worksheet if it is appropriate for their skill level.

3. Have students work together to orally recall all the details from the group activity before they begin drawing.

4. Have students use their individual worksheet to draw a picture of the image they made in their mind and described orally.

5. When their drawings are complete, have students write a description of their drawing at the bottom of the worksheet.

6. Ask students to share their drawings and read their descriptions to each other.

Family Connections

1. Students may try this activity at home by working with family members to create an image of something (it could be the clown, a chocolate cake, or an image that has meaning for their family).

2. Students and other family members can draw the image.

3. Ask some students to write about their image as well as draw it.

4. Have students bring the images to school and describe them to the class.

All Ears for Idioms

Activity Overview

All Ears for Idioms gives students the opportunity to hear and practice listening to, reading, and writing a variety of idiomatic expressions. Idioms show students that flexible understanding is sometimes needed for language comprehension. Idioms appear frequently in our language, so when students don't understand them, they often lose comprehension both orally and in written text. All Ears for Idioms gives students a chance to learn idiomatic expressions and engage in metalinguistic thinking as they compare and contrast what it appears the idiom means versus what it really means.

In this activity, students will first work with the teacher modeling in a group. Then, they'll work with a partner to read and write idioms and draw the concrete interpretation of the idiom as well as the figurative use of it. The more teachers use figurative language in the classroom, the more depth and flexibility their students acquire as they approach text comprehension.

> ## Materials ● ● ● ● ● ● ●
>
> - Sample Idiom List (see Appendix B)
> - Index cards
> - Drawing paper and pencil, crayons, etc.
> - All Ears for Idioms Worksheet (see Appendix A)
> - Props for acting out idioms

Link to Literacy

All Ears for Idioms helps students understand that some phrases in our language need to be thought about flexibly. Knowing the dictionary definition of a vocabulary word is sometimes not enough. Having a depth of knowledge about a word or phrase means understanding that it may be used differently in different situations. For example, being "all ears" does not mean that a person is covered with ears! When students understand language flexibility at the oral level, their reading comprehension can be significantly enhanced.

Whole-Class Activity

Set the purpose. Say: "Learning about idioms is fun because it makes us think about language in new and playful ways. When someone skis well, we might say that skiing is 'a piece of cake for him.' No one has given him a piece of cake, but it means that skiing is really easy for him."

1. Put an idiom on the board, such as **all ears**.

2. Use the idiom in context. **Say:** "When the teacher was talking about who would get extra recess time, the boy was **all ears**."

3. Ask the class if anyone can figure out what it means to be **all ears.**

4. Draw two boxes on the front board. In one box, draw a picture of someone who is literally **all ears** (really big ears or multiple ears). In the other box, draw a picture of someone who is listening attentively to someone else.

5. Ask the class to fidget and not listen while you read a page of a book. Then call them to attention and ask them to be **all ears** as you read the next page of the book.

Return to the purpose. Say: "Learning to think about words in new and playful ways will help you understand idioms when you encounter them in your reading."

Independent/Paired Activity

1. Repeat this activity by writing idioms on index cards, then asking students to choose a card. The card should have an idiom by itself and also a sentence in which the idiom is used within context so students can interpret and understand its meaning (e.g., raining cats and dogs; The children couldn't go out to play because it was raining cats and dogs outside.).

2. Put students into pairs. Give each student an All Ears for Idioms Worksheet.

3. Have students work together to figure out the meaning of the idiom with their partner.

4. On their worksheets, ask students to each draw two pictures, one for the literal meaning ("what it sounds like it means") and one for the figurative meaning ("what it really means"). Their drawings can be different from each others, or they can decide on the same examples and draw individual versions of the same examples on their worksheets.

5. Have students create a little skit to act out both meanings of the idiom.

6. Give students an opportunity to share their "idiom skits" with the whole group.

Family Connections

1. Send home a list of three idioms and have students ask their parents or family members to help them come up with a sentence for each that will be shared in class the next day.

2. Have students ask their parents or family members if they can think of another idiom.

Chatterboxes

Activity Overview

Chatterboxes is an activity that uses the discovery of objects, pictures, or topic cards to stimulate discussion. The activity makes use of new stimuli to motivate students to effectively label and describe pictures or objects, elaborate on the descriptions, and have conversations about them. The activity can also serve as a starter for developing foundations to compose simple written responses to different objects, pictures, or topics.

Materials • • • • • •

- Attractive box with objects in it (Chatterbox 1)
- Attractive box with word cards and pictures that connect to the words (Chatterbox 2)
- Attractive box with topic cards and pictures that represent the topics (Chatterbox 3)

Link to Literacy

Oral response, to either a simple picture of a child playing at the beach or a more complex picture of individuals casting their ballots at a polling place, can act as a developmental bridge, enhancing students' ability to respond to similar concepts when they are encountered in text.

Whole-Class Activity

Set the purpose. Say: "You are going to have fun choosing things to talk about. When you speak about the objects or pictures you discover, you can become better speakers, and as you listen to each other, you can become better listeners."

1. Choose students one at a time.

2. Let each take a turn at opening Chatterbox 1, 2, or 3 and removing an object, picture, or topic card.

3. As the first student takes something from one of the Chatterboxes, have the student announce what it is. Call on a second student to describe the object, its use, or its purpose. Then, call on a third student to use the word in a sentence. For example, the first student takes a picture or object representing a dog out of the Chatterbox and says, "It's a dog." The second student says, "A dog is a pet." The third student says, "I have a dog at my house and her name is Rosie." (Another approach is to have one student complete all three tasks.)

4. (This next step uses the skill developed in the Buddy Talk activity.) Tell all the students to find their Talking Buddy (this can be someone you have selected or it can be random).

5. Have each student create a sentence that taps into their background knowledge about the Chatterbox word chosen previously, in this case, their knowledge about dogs.

Chatterboxes

47

6. These steps can be repeated using the other Chatterboxes. This activity can be done with simple objects or with more advanced, grade-appropriate content material. For example, at a higher level, a student may choose a picture of a cradleboard or a tipi from Chatterbox 2 in reference to a social studies theme. This is a highly variable activity and depends on the age and needs of your students.

Return to the purpose. Say: "You have been speaking about objects and pictures or topics you have discovered. This kind of practice can help you become better speakers and listeners. It will also help you understand what you hear and read, and help you to write about things you want to write about."

Independent/Paired Activity I

Easy Version

1. Students work with a partner or Talking Buddy.

2. Students choose three objects randomly from Chatterbox 1 or three picture cards from Chatterbox 2. For example:

3. Have students create one or two sentences together that incorporate all the objects they chose, such as: *The dog buried his bone under the bed. The brown and white dog buried his bone under the blue bed.*

Advanced Version

1. Choose a student who will pick a topic with a picture from Chatterbox 3.

2. Have the student read the topic out loud to the class, show its corresponding picture, and then make a statement about the topic. For example, if the topic was the American Revolution, the student could say, "The colonists fought for their independence during the American Revolution."

3. Have the first student choose a second student. Ask that student to add his or her own sentence to the topic, such as "Patrick Henry was a patriot who fought in the American Revolution."

4. Ask if another student can repeat both sentences.

5. Repeat the activity by having another student add to the original sentence or pick a new topic from Chatterbox 3.

Independent /Paired Activity II

1. Have students work with partners. Let them choose objects, topics, or words from the Chatterboxes (1, 2, or 3).

2. Have students discuss the topics, objects, or words.

3. Have students draw or find other pictures to illustrate the topic, object, or word they chose.

4. Have students each write a sentence, a few sentences, or a paragraph (depending on skill level) about the topic, object, or word.

Family Connections

1. Have students bring an object from Chatterbox 1 home for discussion with a family member.

2. Have students ask a family member to create a sentence about the object or simply talk to them about the object.

3. Have students write down the sentence or some of the information generated by their family member.

4. If the family member does not speak English, the student can share the sentence with the class by writing it on the board in the other language in order to enhance the other students' knowledge of different cultures and languages.

Chatterboxes

Flyswatter Sentences

Activity Overview

The Flyswatter Sentences activity encourages student fluency through the use of receptive and expressive vocabulary. Receptive vocabulary refers to the words a student can recognize when listening, but not necessarily use yet. Expressive vocabulary refers to the words a student actually uses when speaking and writing. This activity also allows students to practice sentence formation and using words in context.

Students work in teams to recognize, produce, define, and apply target (academic) words in a fluent manner. Using flyswatters, students try to be the first person to "swat" the correct word, answer a question, or use it in a sentence.

Materials • • • • • • •

- ◎ Flyswatters
- ◎ Flyswatter Sentences Worksheet (see Appendix A)
- ◎ Picture index cards that represent target vocabulary words
- ◎ Picture index cards that align with concepts that are taught in your curriculum

Link to Literacy

Vocabulary is an important factor in both oral and written comprehension. Knowing words well enough to retrieve and apply them in context is an important skill that relates to reading comprehension. The more students know about words, the more likely they will be able to recall, retrieve, and connect those words for accurate and deep reading comprehension, and for writing.

Whole-Class Activity

Set the purpose. Say: "This activity will give you practice in recognizing words quickly and accurately. Becoming automatic with your ability to recognize and use words will help you to understand those words when they appear in books you are reading, and will help you use those words to make your writing more interesting."

1. Divide the class into two teams. Have the teams line up on both sides of the room.

2. Put several picture cards that represent target vocabulary words on the front board. (Enlarge the images if needed so the whole class can see them.) These should all be words that have been taught previously. For older students, write words directly on the board and have students swat a word when they hear information that describes it.

3. Call on one student from each team to approach the front of the room. Give each student a flyswatter.

4. Say, for example, "Swat the picture of something that is used when it is raining." (The student who swats the umbrella first gets one point for his or her team.)

5. Have each student pass the flyswatter to the next student behind him or her. Or, you could ask the team member who did not swat the picture first, "What is it called?" If the student can answer correctly, "It is an umbrella," his or her team gets a point, as well.

6. Use another picture for the next two players or continue working with them on the previous word. For example, say, "Swat the umbrella if you can use that word in a new sentence."

7. This activity can be used with pictures of content from your curriculum. For example, if you are learning about Native Americans, you might use pictures from a social studies book in your classroom, extending the pictures into words, and then applying them to sentences.

Return to the Purpose. Say: "Becoming automatic with your ability to recognize and use words will help you to understand those words when they appear in books you are reading and will help you to use those words to make your writing more interesting."

Independent/Paired Activity

1. Students work in pairs.

2. Give student partners picture cards that represent target words. Ask them to put the stack of cards with the picture face down on their desk.

3. Have the students play a game of "speed" with the cards. To play "speed," have students take turns turning over the top card in the pile. The first one to slap the card and say the word correctly gets a point.

4. Ask the student who didn't get the card the first time to use the word correctly in a sentence. Give the student a point if he or she does this correctly. If he or she cannot, then the student who first named the picture can earn an extra point by using the word in a sentence.

5. Give the student who needs a turn another chance to earn a point by having him or her elaborate on or expand the sentence made by the previous student.

6. After students have gone through their entire deck of picture cards, have them choose two to four words they enjoyed and ask them to create sentences with them. Have them share their sentences with each other.

7. Finally, have students write their chosen words on the Flyswatter Sentences Worksheet, illustrate them, and write their created sentences underneath.

Family Connections

1. If students have not completed their Flyswatter Sentences Worksheets, they can take them home to complete and share with their families.

2. Ask students to explain the target words, and their connection to the words, to their family members.

Flyswatter Sentences

Word Web Sentences

Activity Overview

Word Web Sentences develops a student's ability to enhance and elaborate sentences. It helps students advance from using short, truncated sentences to longer, more complex and descriptive sentences. Relevant words that are related to a topic of study, story, or book study are placed in a word web. The main word is placed in the middle and six related words spoke out from its center. Students touch several words (main and related) and incorporate all of them into a sentence, reinforcing the main word's meaning and further developing their vocabulary.

Materials

- Word Web Sentences Worksheet (see Appendix A) for student use
- Content-related words, both a main word and words that relate to it
- Word Web Sentences Worksheet (see Appendix A) enlarged or enlarged and laminated for teacher use.
- Dry-erase markers
- Magic wands or pointers

Link to Literacy

Word Web Sentences gives students the opportunity to learn how to speak and write more clearly through the creation of word-specific sentences. Students learn to develop their ability to sort and select words in order to find the right one that will help them best express themselves.

Whole-Class Activity

Set the purpose. Say: "If you can understand how words connect with each other, it will help you choose just the right word you are looking for when you speak or write. The more we can use interesting words that connect to each other in our speaking and writing, the more easily we will be able to understand information and make others understand us."

1. Introduce a main word or phrase that students will encounter in reading or content-area study. The word or phrase can come from a story or novel, or a science, math, or social studies unit. Or, make the word reflect other activities that are occurring in your class or school. For example, if your school is involved in a community service project, you could choose the word **philanthropic**. Be sure to give students a good definition and a good example of the word. Generate a few other examples from the class.

2. Put the enlarged and laminated Word Web Sentences Worksheet on the front board (or draw a web).

3. Write the main word **philanthropic** in the middle of the radial word web and generate other related words that can be placed in the outer, connected circles all around it (e.g., **service**, **give**, **help**, **community**, **donate**, **collect**, **needy**, **respect**, **enhance**, **support**).

Vocabulary Development Activities

4. Model creating a sentence by touching each target word in your sentence as you use the words. You can literally slap each word as you say it, or you can use a pointer or magic wand to point to each word as you incorporate it into your sentence. Say, for example, "Our school is **collecting** money for **needy** students in another **community**, and that is **philanthropic**." Write the sentence beneath the word web.

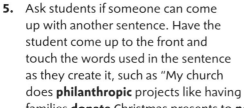

5. Ask students if someone can come up with another sentence. Have the student come up to the front and touch the words used in the sentence as they create it, such as "My church does **philanthropic** projects like having families **donate** Christmas presents to **needy** families in our **community**."

6. This activity discourages the formation of short sentences such as "I collected books." Students have the words in front of them, and the selection process becomes just as important as the sentence-formation process.

7. Have students get up and find a "Talking Buddy" just as they did in the previous Buddy Talk activity.

8. Have students tell their buddy something that they have participated in that was philanthropic in nature.

9. Have them move on to another buddy and share the philanthropic experience of their first partner with their second partner. Remember that this second step encourages purposeful listening.

Return to the purpose. Say: "Knowing words that are connected will help you create really interesting sentences as you share your ideas with others."

Independent/Paired Activity

1. Keep students in their "Talking Buddy" pairs.

2. Give student pairs Word Web Sentences Worksheets and ask them to fill them out, using either the same main word you modeled for them, or another main word driven by content that will develop essential, domain-specific background knowledge.

3. Have student pairs work together to fill out the related word portion of their individual worksheets.

4. Ask student pairs to create two sentences each by touching the words they use on their worksheets as they create their sentences.

5. Have them share their sentences with their partner orally and then write the sentences they have created on their worksheet.

Family Connections

1. Have students take a Word Web Sentences Worksheet home and discuss the main word **philanthropic** with their family. For example, they can ask, "When have you helped someone else in need?"

2. Have students fill out the worksheet by putting in relevant words for their family. Have them create a sentence together with their family members with these words. For example: "In my office, we all **contribute** so we can buy turkeys to **help** families that cannot afford to buy one at Thanksgiving."

3. Have students share their webs in class the next day.

Living Concept Maps

Activity Overview

The Living Concept Maps activity supports student language development through the creation of a "living graphic organizer" that acts as a thinking map. Concept maps are graphic representations that make concepts easier to understand and remember by sorting them into the main idea, subcategories, and supporting details. This activity gets students actively engaged in the concepts that are being taught and analyzed. Students have fun becoming a part of a physical concept map. Some students may have seen graphic organizers for years on paper but tend to see them as simply another worksheet. They may use them aimlessly without making any deep connection with the concepts they are designed to represent. Creating a "living concept map" helps students experience how useful a graphic organizer can be as it assists in organizing their thinking and then their words, both orally and in preparation for writing.

Materials

- Card stock or chart paper
- Markers
- Index cards
- Masking tape
- Self-stick notes and file folders
- Family Homework Note (see Appendix B)

Link to Literacy

The Living Concept Maps activity supports comprehension both orally and in reading, and assists in the organization and preparation of written work. By participating in the creation of a physical representation of the ideas being organized, students begin to understand what is meant by a main idea, subcategories, and supporting details.

Whole-Class Activity I

Set the purpose. Say: "Using a concept map can help you organize your thoughts and ideas and can make learning easier. Today you are going to create a concept map based on a story you have been reading or the topic you have been studying. The concept map will help you think about and understand the story more clearly."

This activity can be done at many different grade levels with narrative and expository text and content-area topics of study. The sample story for this concept map is "Tim's Buddy," a decodable text from *Power Readers* by Susan Ebbers (2007). Concept maps can be drawn in many different styles. For example:

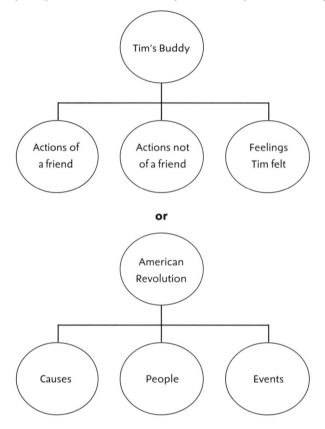

1. Decide on three categories (e.g., main idea or topic, themes, and events) that will be included in the concept map. This step can be done with the class or you can prepare it ahead of time. Write the categories on card stock to make "category cards."

2. Draw the concept map on the front board and explain the categories to the class.

3. Give students index cards (the number will depend on students' ability level) for creating a concept map. At the beginning of a unit of study you might want to give out index cards with words that will fit into various categories you are about to study. As an informal, end-of-study assessment, you might want to give students blank index cards and let them generate words that will fit into the various categories you just studied. For this example, students will have index cards with either the "Actions of a friend," "Actions not of a friend," or "Feelings Tim felt."

4. Clear a space in the classroom for students to stand. Move desks if needed to accommodate the whole class.

5. Give the category cards to some of your students and have them stand in the same pattern as the concept map drawn on the front board.

6. Ask the rest of the class to line up behind, or group themselves around, the subcategories of the concept map according to their index cards. For instance, students who have "Actions of a friend" will group by the student who is holding up that concept card.

7. You can also call on students one at a time to read their index card and direct them to line up behind the appropriate concept map category.

8. Eventually all students will become part of the concept map.

Return to the purpose. Say: "Creating the concept map with your bodies helps you to understand and remember important ideas more easily."

Whole-Class Activity II

For this portion of the activity, use this concept map as an example:

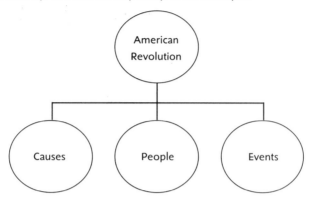

Sentence Creation and Combining

1. Ask students who are creating the concept map to use their word in context in a sentence about this subcategory. For example, a student who wrote **freedom** on their index card as a "cause" subcategory of the American Revolution might say, "One of the causes of the American Revolution is that the colonists wanted their freedom."

2. Repeat this exercise until all students have created sentences.

3. You might ask some students if they can use two of their words in a simple sentence. For example, "The desire for lower taxes and freedom were causes of the American Revolution."

4. If students have had direct instruction in the use of conjunctions, you can ask them to take two of the sentences that have been created (by themselves or their classmates) and combine them using a conjunction. For example: "The colonists wanted their freedom and were willing to fight against England to win their independence."

Living Concept Maps

Writing Extensions

Depending on the level of your class, there are other activity extensions (e.g., the paragraph outline, essay writing) that are very effective to do at this point.

Paragraph Outline

Model writing a paragraph outline with the concept map for students:

- ◎ The card with the main idea is the basis of the topic sentence.

- ◎ The three subcategory cards represent the three detail sentences.

- ◎ The closing sentence is created by referring back to the main topic.

Topic sentence: The colonists began a war for independence called the American Revolution.
First detail: Many brave people fought in the war, such as George Washington and Paul Revere.
Second detail: There were fierce battles between the colonists and the English soldiers.
Third detail: The colonists fought for many causes, but especially for their independence from England.
Closing sentence: At the end of the American Revolution, the colonists were victorious over the English and America became a free and independent country.

Essay Writing

Model writing a five-paragraph essay outline with the concept map for students:

- ◎ The introductory paragraph starts with a topic sentence, and then is based on the main idea and an overview of the subcategories.

- ◎ The three detail paragraphs are generated from the subcategories and the details. For example, one paragraph is about the causes of the American Revolution, one is about the people involved, and the third is about the events of that time.

- ◎ The closing paragraph is a summary of the important details and references to the original introductory paragraph and the topic sentence.

Independent/Paired Activity

1. Students will work with partners and each partner will recreate the concept map done in the group activity in a folder using self-stick notes (one for the main idea, three for the subcategories, several for the detail words under the subcategories).

2. Have students choose three to five of the words they created for the concept map subcategories.

3. Have students take turns creating sentences and sharing them with each other, or ask them to work together to come up with good sentences.

4. Have students write the sentences they have created.

5. If age appropriate, ask students to create a paragraph, together or individually, and write their sentences in paragraph structure. Students can put their sentences on sentence strips first and then create the paragraph by assembling the strips and then rewriting their paragraph on a piece of writing paper.

6. If age appropriate, ask students to create an essay, together or individually, based on the concept map. Have students follow the structure they were taught previously.

Family Connections

1. Have students bring their concept map home and explain it to their family.

2. Ask students to bring back a Family Homework Note for the concept map. Ask them to answer the questions and have a family member sign it.

Learning From Proverbs

Activity Overview

Proverbs are popular sayings that offer advice and wisdom or state a culturally accepted truth. Ben Franklin wrote American proverbs about thriftiness and the rewards of hard work, island cultures have proverbs about the sea, and African proverbs often involve animals. Proverbs are usually passed down through the generations orally and are generally simple and easy to remember, because they are short and can connect personally with their meanings. This makes proverbs perfect tools for teaching oral language.

The Learning From Proverbs activity motivates students to work out the meanings of these unique sayings. To do so, students must share their own experiences and ideas while listening to those of others. In this activity, students begin by listening to proverbs, then talking about them, acting them out, and finally, drawing them, as they deepen their understanding of the words.

Materials ......

- Proverbs List (see Appendix B)
- Proverbs written on index cards
- Drawing paper, writing paper, pencil, and crayons
- Plastic sheet protectors
- Camera

Link to Literacy

Some phrases in our language need to be thought about flexibly. The Learning From Proverbs activity helps students understand that, often, knowing the dictionary definition of vocabulary words is not enough. Having a depth of knowledge about a word or phrase means understanding that it may be used differently in different situations. Studying and using proverbs can help build and expand students' linguistic background knowledge while they practice their oral language skills.

Whole-Class Activity

Set the purpose. Say: "Learning about proverbs is fun because it makes you think about language in new and interesting ways."

1. Put this proverb on the board: "Don't cry over spilt milk."

2. Use the proverb in context: "Danny cried after he lost his watch and his mother said, 'Don't cry over spilt milk.'"

3. Ask the class if anyone can figure out what Danny's mother meant when she told him not to cry over spilt milk. **Say:** "Did Danny spill milk and lose his watch? Will that proverb help Danny to feel better about his situation?"

4. If students cannot figure it out, then teach the meaning directly.

Learning From Proverbs

59

5. Ask several students to share an example of their own when they "cried over spilt milk."

6. Sit in a circle and create a progressive oral story. You start, then have a student to your right add a sentence, and so on, until the story is finished. For example, start by telling what caused Danny to cry. Then tell what happened after his mother told him not to cry over spilt milk. After several students have taken turns ask, "How will the story end?"

7. Have students return to their desks. The next portion of the activity can be done on the same day or over several days. Write the proverb, "two heads are better than one," on the board and draw a two-headed monster beside it.

8. Ask the class to figure out what the proverb might really mean.

9. Call two students up to the front of the room and have them put their heads close together in any way they want to put them (e.g., chin to crown of head, right side to left side, see the picture below). Ask the class to guess the proverb now that they see it.

Tell the students that everyone will get a chance to act out proverbs like this.

Return to the purpose. Say: "It is fun to 'play with words' and think about what they really mean. Thinking flexibly about words can make you a better writer."

Independent/Paired Activity I

While students are working on this activity, write all the proverbs they are using on the front board.

1. Have students work in small groups or pairs depending on what you think will work best.

2. Put proverbs and their meanings on two sides of an index card (proverb on one side and meaning on the other). Give each group or pair a card.

3. Ask students to discuss what they think the proverb really means before turning the card over. When they have made a decision, they can check their thoughts by looking at the answer on the back of the card.

4. Ask students to work together and figure out a way to act out their proverb. For example, they may do the following for the proverb, "In unity there is strength".

5. Have students take turns acting out their proverbs for the rest of the class.

6. Have students who are not acting watch and try to guess which proverb is being demonstrated. To help guessing, tell students to look at the front board (where you have written all the possible proverbs) and choose from one of the proverbs.

7. Use your camera to take pictures of students while they are acting out the proverbs. Later, you can make a Learning From Proverbs bulletin board and put the proverbs, and the students' photos demonstrating their proverbs, on the board.

Independent/Paired Activity II

1. Have students create an Illustrated Proverb Book with a proverb and its definition on one page, and an illustration and description of the proverb on the opposite page.

2. Students will share their proverb books with other students, so ask them to include a sentence that describes each illustration, while using the proverb.

3. Have students each choose a proverb and create a Proverb Book that makes the proverb a central part of the story, similar to the Danny story illustrated previously.

Family Connections

1. Have students take home a list of the proverbs they have learned in class (place the list in a plastic sheet protector to keep it neat).

2. Have students ask their family members about a time in their lives when one of the proverbs was true for them.

3. Have students ask family members for additional proverbs not on the Proverbs List. (Encourage students to share these proverbs with the class as a way of expanding all students' cultural and language understanding.)

4. When students complete their Proverb Book, have them share it with their families.

Learning From Proverbs

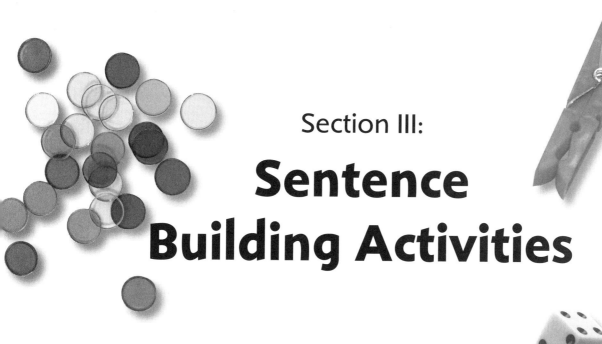

Section III:
Sentence Building Activities

Learning to speak, unlike learning to read, appears to be a natural process. Students learn to speak by living in an environment that exposes them to words. However, the degree to which children have been exposed to rich vocabulary and complex syntax varies. When students come to school with a lack of exposure to rich oral language it is our job to wash them in the wonderful words and language they have been missing. One of the best ways to do this is to read to your class. Reading to students often exposes them to more interesting and beautiful language than they might hear you use regularly in the classroom. Allowing students to hear complex language sets the stage for them to learn to understand it, both orally and in text, and gives them the chance to use it themselves in oral communication and writing.

The activities in this section are designed to help students grow in their ability to speak in complete sentences. Each activity increases in difficulty so that students begin by learning grammatically correct structures for basic sentences and, eventually, are taught to expand their sentences in order to communicate more clearly and fully, both orally and in writing.

ABC... Talk to Me

Activity Overview

ABC...Talk to Me is a simple activity that stimulates listening, sentence creation, and elaboration. Sometimes students are reluctant or unable to speak in complete sentences. This activity will give students the practice they need in order to become comfortable with lengthier sentences and more complex syntax. This added language exposure will help them become accustomed to the language they will eventually encounter in reading.

ABC...Talk to Me gives students practice with the concept of subject, predicate, noun, and verb. In a simple activity, students begin to create and elaborate sentences using their awareness of grammatical sentence structure and the requirement of subject and predicate. This activity is easily adaptable—you can take a few phoneme/grapheme correspondences that you are working on in class and use them with this activity. Two students can also work together during the activity (coming up with sentences together or taking turns choosing new words to incorporate into their responses).

Materials • • • • • •

- ABC. . . Talk to Me Word List (see Appendix A)
- Pocket Chart
- Drawing paper
- Index cards (picture cards if appropriate) called noun and verb cards, made with words and/or pictures on them from the Word List words you choose (have a good mix of nouns and verbs represented, mount the nouns and verbs on different color cards)
- Objects

Link to Literacy

Texts that students read are not just made up of simple sentences. They may have many variations of complex syntax with which students are not familiar. ABC...Talk to Me gets students engaged in the creation of sentences that start out simple but may become increasingly complex as they choose to use more words.

Whole-Class Activity

Set the Purpose. Say: "You are going to be creating sentences with pictures you choose. When you use good sentences when you talk, it helps you to become better speakers and readers, and to understand other people who also use good sentences."

1. Arrange preselected picture cards in a pocket chart. You may choose to select pictures that reinforce a particular phoneme you are teaching. In so doing, you will create extra practice in hearing and using that phoneme in words. An approach for older students is to use

pictures that represent a variety of nouns and verbs without attention to consistency of initial phonemes.

2. **Say:** "Good sentences have at least two parts to them. One part is about someone or something. It is called the **subject**. The other part is about what that person or thing is doing. It is called the **predicate**."

3. Write the sentence, *The girl is listening*, on the board. **Say:** "An example of a good sentence is: *The girl is listening*. It has two parts. Can you find the two parts?"

4. Ask for a student volunteer to come up to the board and find the part about someone or something (the subject). Have the student put a circle around that part of the sentence. (If students cannot read yet, then ask the question orally and have them simply answer, "**the girl**.")

5. Repeat this for the second part of the sentence, the predicate. **Say:** "Who can find the part that tells what the girl is doing?" Ask for a student volunteer to come up and put a squiggly line under that part of the sentence.

6. Now, model choosing some of the pictures you have arranged in the pocket chart. **Say:** "I have picked from the pictures that start with the sound /f/. I am going to pick two pictures that are about someone or something, so I will pick **a fox** and I will pick the picture of someone using **a fishing pole**. All the pictures in the pocket chart are either nouns or verbs. Nouns are naming words. They name people, places, and things. Verbs are doing words. They tell about what the people are doing. All subjects are nouns, but nouns don't have to be subjects, etc.

7. Make a sentence with those two words. **Say:** "The fox is fishing." Ask if a student volunteer can identify the two parts of the sentence.

8. Keep the fishing part and ask a student to pick another noun card. For example, if the student picked a picture of a **fairy**, ask the student to build a bigger sentence than the one you made by adding **fairy** to your sentence. The student might create: *The fox and the fairy went fishing*. Your student has just made a sentence with a compound subject.

9. Repeat this activity, writing the sentences on the board.

10. Illustrating sentences can deepen students' engagement with building them. Illustrate one or two of the sentences you wrote on the board. Give out drawing paper and ask students to draw a picture of one of the sentences you made as a group.

Return to the purpose. Say: "You have been creating your own sentences based on the pictures you chose. Your sentences were all about someone who did something. They all had a subject, the person who was doing something, and a predicate, the part that told what the person did. Being able to talk and use great sentences will help you to be better speakers and readers, and it will help you to understand other people who also use good sentences."

Independent/Paired Activity

1. Students who can read and write can do this activity with a partner using picture cards and word cards.

2. If students cannot read and write yet, they should use picture cards only and may need more guidance from the teacher.

3. Give each pair of students ten cards. Remember that picture cards can represent nouns or verbs and word cards can represent nouns or verbs. Offer a mix of both for your students.

4. Ask students to divide the cards into two piles—one for nouns and one for verbs.

5. Working together, have students turn over one noun card and one verb card, and begin to make sentences. Once they have made two or three sentences, have them turn over a second noun card or a second verb card and add to their original sentences, making them into complex sentences.

6. Have the students write their sentences if they can. If they cannot, have them say their sentences and draw them when they are finished creating them.

7. When they are done with their drawings, ask them to look at their drawing and recall their sentence.

8. Ask more advanced students the following questions: "Does your sentence have two parts?" "What are the parts?" "Which is the part about someone or something?" Remind them that we call that part of the sentence the subject. "Which is the part that tells what they are doing?" Remind them that we call that part of the sentence the predicate.

Family Connections

1. Have students take home several picture cards so they can build sentences at home.

2. Have students use the formula for sentence grammar that they have learned depending on grade level.

3. Have students explain to family members that sentences need a subject and a predicate. Let them use these three examples:

    a. sentence = *The man eats*. the subject = the man; the predicate = eats

    b. sentence = *The man reads*. the subject = the man; the predicate = reads

    c. sentence = *The dog eats*. the subject = the dog; the predicate = eats

4. Ask students to work with family members to make three sentences from different combinations (noun and verb) of picture cards.

5. Have students underline the subject in one color and circle the predicate in another color.

Magnetic Sentences

Activity Overview

Magnetic Sentences is an engaging activity that motivates students to develop their ability to enhance and elaborate sentences. It encourages students to move from using short, truncated sentences to longer, more complex, descriptive sentences through the use of magnetic "word" discs and a magnetic wand. Your students will want to be the one to build the longest, most elaborate sentence in order to add more "word" discs to their sentence.

Materials ● ● ● ● ● ● ●

- Magnetic wands and discs
- Magnetic Sentences Tracking Mat (see Appendix A)
- Plastic sheet protectors
- Dry-erase markers
- Overhead projector
- Preselected passage at appropriate reading skill level

Link to Literacy

Magnetic Sentences develops students' ability to create more complex sentences in response to a prompt. Students' ability to comprehend longer sentences, both orally and in text, is related to their ability to use and understand longer and more complex sentences orally.

Whole-Class Activity

Set the purpose. Say: "We are going to be practicing building bigger sentences. When you can create longer and more interesting sentences by yourself, it will help you understand longer sentences when you are listening and reading. It will also make it easier for you to be better at writing down what you want to say."

1. Distribute magnetic wands, discs, and Magnetic Sentences Tracking Mats (in plastic sheet protectors) to students.

2. Model using your own wand, discs, and an overhead projector, if you are doing this with a large group. If you are doing this with a small group, you may model on the table in front of you using your own tracking mat, discs, and wand.

3. Create a short sentence, such as: *I like to read books*, and place a magnetic marker to represent each word of the sentence in a box of the tracking mat, starting at the top, going left to right. Say the sentence to the class. Have them repeat it orally while you touch each disc as they say the sentence together.

4. Repeat the sentence once more, but this time map the sentence by writing each word in a box below the marker—saying the word as they write it. Put a finger under each word as you touch the word and say the sentence.

5. Take the magnetic wand and, moving from left to right, repeat the sentence one more time as you sweep the discs onto the wand.

6. Now, have students use their individual mats as you create magnetic sentences together.

7. Have them repeat this activity themselves using the same sentence you modeled, *I like to read books*.

8. Ask students if they can make the sentence longer. For example, have them create sentences such as: *I like to read books about dogs* or *I like to read picture books about dogs*. Ask questions that help to stimulate and structure the enhancement of their sentences. **Say:** "What kind of dogs do you like to read about?" (*I like to read books about big dogs*.)

9. As an additional part of this activity, you could also have students' color-code the sentence's noun(s) and verb with different-colored discs or use different-colored markers for the words.

10. After students have created their sentences, have them touch and say each word of the sentence with their wands, sweeping up all their magnetic discs.

Return to the purpose. Say: "Building bigger sentences can help you say everything you want to say. When you can speak in longer sentences, it will help you to understand longer sentences when listening and reading. It will also make it easier for you to write down everything you want to say in your writing."

Independent/Paired Activity

1. Students work with a partner.

2. Give students magnetic wands, discs, Magnetic Sentences Tracking Mats, and dry-erase markers.

3. Give students a book or passage that they have already read, or a new one that is at their correct reading level.

4. Have students read the passage, then choose a sentence from the text and read and repeat the sentence together.

5. Have students work together to map the sentence using their tracking mat and discs, writing the words in the row beneath the row with the discs.

6. A second approach, for more advanced students, is to have them read the passage, then take turns creating a sentence that is related to the topic. For example, if one student's original sentence is: *Martin Luther King is a hero*, the new sentence could be: *Martin Luther King now has a holiday that honors him on his birthday*.

7. A second approach, for younger students, could be to create simpler sentences. For example, if one student's original sentence is: *Pam has a cat for a pal*, the new sentence could be: *Pam has a cat named Sam for a pal*.

Family Connections

1. Have parents use wands and discs during back-to-school night, or at a parent education workshop, so they are familiar with the materials and technique.

2. If appropriate for your class situation, have students bring an extra wand, discs, and tracking mat home to work on creating sentences with their family. Students can return the materials the next day.

Clothesline Sentences

Activity Overview

Clothesline Sentences is an activity that can help to develop a student's ability to create and elaborate sentences. The ability to move from the use of short, truncated sentences to longer, more complex and descriptive sentences takes structured and intentional practice. In addition, because this activity is done orally it also enhances purposeful listening and speaking.

Students create sentences with index cards (or cards shaped like pieces of clothing) that each have a word on them. The cards are pinned on a clothesline which is hung up in the classroom. Words can be added, substituted, and manipulated as they hang "on the line." The sentences can also be written on a Clothesline Sentences Worksheet.

Materials

- Multicolored index cards
- Clothing Template (see Appendix B) (copy onto cardstock and laminate)
- Clothesline Sentences Worksheet (see Appendix A)
- Clothesline
- Clothespins
- White board

Link to Literacy

Clothesline Sentences enhances students' ability to create more complex sentences in response to a prompt. Students' ability to comprehend longer sentences in text is related to their ability to use longer and more complex sentences orally. The complexity of language that students hear regularly, and can create on their own, impacts the complexity of material they can read, comprehend, and produce in their writing.

Whole-Class Activity

Set the purpose. Say: "This activity will help you learn to speak in long and interesting sentences. When you can speak in longer sentences, it helps you understand longer sentences when you read and creates good sentences when you write."

Create clothesline sentences that either incorporate a specific subject you have been studying (science or history) or relate to a story that you have read aloud or as a group.

1. Model the technique for your students. Create a sentence within the criteria mentioned and make a line on the front board to represent a clothesline. You could also put an actual clothesline on a wall, or by the front board, and use real clothespins and the Clothing Template to create "clothing word cards".

Clothesline Sentences

2. Write each word of your sentence on laminated, magnetic index "clothing" cards. For example, if your sentence is *The Plains Indians hunted*, each word (**The**, **Plains**, **Indians**, and **hunted**) would be written on their own card.

3. "Hang" laminated, magnetic index "clothing" cards on the front board clothesline.

4. Ask the group if anyone can expand your sentence. For example: *The Plains Indians hunted buffalo*. Add a card with the new word **buffalo** on it. Elaborate the sentence further. **Say:** *The Plains Indians hunted buffalo for food*. Add extra cards for each word and point out how much longer the sentence became—from five words to fifteen.

5. Ask the students what additional information they learned from the expanded sentence.

6. This activity can also be done using color coding (either colored index cards or colored writing on the white cards). The main idea is to code the concept that you want to emphasize for this lesson. For example, the extra words in the elaborated sentence could be placed on laminated cards of a color different than white. Nouns could be one color and verbs another. Adjectives, adverbs, or transition words could be different colors. You decide what you will code. In one lesson you may want to code transition words by placing them on yellow, green, or pink cards, while another time, nouns and verbs might be grammatical concepts that receive purple lettering on white cards. Or, if students write their completed sentences on a white board, have them underline new words with a particular color to align their writing with your coding.

7. This activity is not designed to be the first level of direct instruction for the concepts you are teaching. Rather, it is an opportunity for students to notice, apply, and practice those concepts orally and in written sentences.

Return to the purpose. Say: "Creating bigger and better sentences will make you better speakers, readers, and writers."

Independent/Paired Activity

1. Students work at their desks, using the Clothesline Sentences Worksheet.

2. Have students create a sentence based on the topic you have been discussing. This can be adjusted for students who have difficulty with oral sentence formulation. These students may want to revisit their text and choose a sentence they will copy out of the book and on to their worksheet.

3. Have students take index "clothing" cards and copy the sentence, one word at a time, from the worksheet on to the cards.

4. Have students work with a partner sitting next to them.

5. Have the students mix up their cards and have their partners unscramble them to create and read the sentence.

Sentence Building Activities

6. Have the students pick up their sentence cards and place them, using clothespins, on the clothesline in the classroom.

Family Connections

1. Have students take their clothesline sentences and make a copy on a second set of index cards.

2. Have them take this set home and ask someone in their family to unscramble the words to make a sentence.

3. If parents speak a different language, students can take home another set of index cards for a translation of the first set. Students can share the translation with the class by writing it on the board next to their original sentence. This step will honor the student's home language and increase the exposure of the class to different languages and cultures.

Clothesline Sentences

Chain-Link Sentences

Activity Overview

The ability to be comfortable reading and understanding longer, more complex sentences begins with the ability to create more complex sentences orally. Many students speak in short, truncated sentences, so when they encounter longer sentences, either orally in the classroom while their teacher is speaking or in books that they are reading, the syntax may seem unfamiliar and the complexity and lack of familiarity can interfere with comprehension.

Chain-Link Sentences motivates students to develop their own ability to enhance and elaborate sentences. It encourages students to move from using short sentences to longer, more complex and descriptive sentences. Students write words on paper chain links. The longer their sentence is, the more links they can put on their chain. Nouns, verbs, and other parts of speech may be written on different color links to denote their special job in the sentence. Subjects and predicates can also be written on different color links to demonstrate the grammatical structure of the sentence, depending on the focus of instruction.

Materials • • • • • • •

- Paper chain-links
- Plastic sheet protectors
- Dry-erase markers
- Chain-Link Sentences Worksheet (see Appendix A)
- Overhead projector

Link to Literacy

Chain-Link Sentences develops students' ability to create more complex sentences in response to a prompt. Students' ability to comprehend longer sentences in text is related to their ability to use and understand longer and more complex sentences orally.

Whole-Class Activity

Set the purpose. Say: "We are going to be practicing building bigger sentences. When you can create longer and more interesting sentences yourself, you'll understand longer sentences when you are listening and reading. And, you will also become better at writing down what you want to say."

Create chain-link sentences that either incorporate a specific subject you have been studying (science or history) or relate to a story you have read as a group.

1. Put the Chain-Link Sentences Worksheet on an overhead projector.

2. Model the technique of creating a sentence on the Chain-Link Sentences Worksheet.

3. Write each word of your sentence, *The boy rides his bike*, in one of the ovals (chain-links) with a dry-erase marker. Skip occasional ovals to leave space for future sentence building.

4. Ask the group if anyone can expand your sentence. For example, a student might say, "The little boy rides his red bike," or, "Tim rides his new bike down the big hill." Add the new-words in the appropriate oval chain-links, adding links as needed.

5. Ask students what additional information they learned from the expanded sentence.

6. This activity can also be done with color-coded chain-links or colored markers used for nouns, verbs, or conjunctions. The main idea is to code the concept that you want to emphasize for this lesson. For example, in one lesson you may want to code transition words, but another time nouns and verbs might receive color coding.

7. Distribute Chain-Link Sentences Worksheets (placed in plastic sheet protectors) and dry-erase markers to students. Ask someone to create a sentence. Model by writing it on the board (or overhead transparency) and have students follow your placement of the words in the chain-links.

Return to the purpose. Say: "Building bigger sentences can help you to say everything you want to say. When you can speak in longer sentences, it will be easier for you to understand longer sentences when you are listening and reading. And, it will make it easier for you to express everything you want to in your writing."

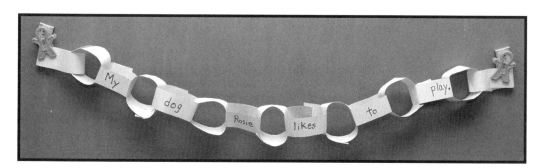

Independent /Paired Activity

1. Students work with a partner, using their Chain-Link Sentences Worksheets and dry-erase markers.

2. Give students a book or passage they have already read, or a new one that is at their correct reading level.

3. Have students read the passage and then choose a sentence from the text and read and repeat the sentence together.

4. Ask students to work together to write the sentence, putting their words link by link, on their worksheet.

5. For more advanced students, have them read the passage, then take turns creating a sentence that is related to the topic. For example, if the original sentence is: *The firemen used special equipment to fight the fire*, one student's new sentence could be: *Firemen use special fireproof clothes to protect themselves when they fight fires.*

6. For younger students, have them create simpler sentences. For example, if the original sentence is: *John took his pet to the vet*, one student's new sentence could be: *John took his sick pup, Penny, to the vet.*

Chain-Link Sentences

7. After students have written their initial sentences, encourage them to elaborate further, growing longer and longer sentences. Give students the opportunity to listen to the sentence, repeat it aloud, and then add to it.

8. Another way that this can be done is to encourage the use of particular grammatical constructions in the new sentence. For example, ask students to add an adjective, an adverb, or a conjunction to their new sentence. This is an activity that reinforces previous direct instruction of specific concepts and gives students an opportunity to practice using those concepts orally and in written sentences.

9. Have students differentiate the targeted grammatical concept with a differently colored marker or a paper chain-link made of a different color.

Family Connections

1. Have students take home paper for making chain-link sentences at home.

2. Ask students to create sentences that are based on something they have talked about for 30 seconds or longer with a family member.

Growing Sentence Stems

Activity Overview

Growing Sentences is an activity that provides added structure for students' attempts at oral sentence formation. It provides sentence starters in the form of sentence stems, out of which bigger sentences can grow. The activity helps students use words to describe ideas they may have in their minds, but have difficulty expressing orally. In addition, students have an opportunity to practice listening to, creating, and writing complete sentences that can be elaborated and combined as they become ready to do so.

Materials • • • • • •

- Sentence starter ideas based on themes, concepts, and text relevant to your class
- Chart paper
- Koosh ball

Link to Literacy

Good readers and writers are more aware of the structure of sentences than poor readers and writers. They are able to revise their sentences to make them better. Direct instruction in sentence structure, plus opportunities to practice creating sentences for speaking and writing, is an important step in the development and improvement of oral language skills. Oral language skills create the foundation for reading comprehension.

Whole-Class Activity I

Set the purpose. Say: "We are going to practice building sentences. We will start with a beginning idea called a stem. Then, we will grow our sentences just like flowers, watching them get bigger and prettier as they grow upon their stems."

1. Write a sentence stem on the board. It should be something that you know will have meaning for your students. Depending on the level of your students it can be quite simple or more complex. For example: *I like to* _____, works well for younger students or students with lower language skills and, *If I could have any wish, it would be* _____, works well for older students.

2. Model one response for the lower-level students. **Say:** "I like to eat mint, chocolate-chip ice cream." Be sure to repeat the sentence as a whole, modeling not just the ending, but the entire sentence in a fluent manner.

3. Ask the students to turn to a neighbor and share how they would end the sentence, then ask them to repeat the whole sentence with their personal ending.

4. Ask a couple of students for their version of the complete sentence.

5. Ask the class to repeat the sentences as you write them on the front board.

6. Reinforce information that has been previously taught directly in your class about the structure of good sentences. For example, if you have been studying nouns and verbs, underline or box those words to draw attention to those concepts.

7. If students are ready instructionally, you could try modeling sentence combining with two of the sentences created. For example, if the sentences were: *I like to eat chocolate ice cream* and *I like to play with my dog*, some possible combinations could be:

   ☺ *I like to eat chocolate ice cream when I play with my dog.*

   ☺ *I like to play with my dog while I eat chocolate ice cream.*

8. Then, ask the students to pick two sentences from the ones written on the board and try combining them. Call on a few students to hear their created sentences.

9. Ask students to get up and move around the room. When you give a signal to stop, have them share their first sentence ending (from Step 3) and repeat their whole sentence to the student they stop near. Have the other student take a turn (e.g., *eat ice cream, I like to eat ice cream*).

10. Ask the students to move on to another student, and, this time, have them share their own sentence, and the sentence of the last person they spoke with. This step promotes active listening as students are asked to recall their first partner's sentence as well as their own.

Return to the purpose. Say: "You have been 'growing' wonderful sentences, and this kind of practice will make you better speakers, readers, and writers."

Whole-Class Activity II

Koosh Ball Sentence Building

1. Use a Koosh ball for student engagement and attention.

2. Have students stand in a circle.

3. Tell students that you are going to build sentences, one word at a time, as you throw the Koosh ball to each other. Every time a student catches the ball, he or she adds a word to the sentence. Each person has to say the words that were said before his turn and then add his words onto the sentence. Then, holding the ball, he or she will repeat the whole sentence.

4. For students who have difficulty with sentence construction it is a good idea to start with a sentence stem about something that the class knows and cares about. For example, if you have been studying Native Americans in class, you may have a sentence that starts with: *The Plains Indians liked to* _____, or: *Some woodland animals eat* _____.

5. Throw the Koosh ball to the first student, state the sentence stem, and ask the student to add one word or phrase to the sentence. For example: *"If I had one wish + it would be that = If I had one wish it would be that* _____." The first student throws the ball to the next student. The next student repeats the sentence so far then adds his or her own words. For example: *"If I had one wish it would be that ... I could eat ice cream every day. = If I had one wish it would be that I could eat ice cream every day."*

6. Have the entire group repeat the sentence chorally.

7. Write the sentence on a piece of chart paper for review later.

8. Do the activity again with the same sentence starter so that more students get to participate. Whenever it is appropriate, change the sentence starter and begin again.

Independent/Paired Activity

1. Students will work with a partner.

2. Ask students to choose one of the sentences you have written on the board or chart paper and copy it onto a blank piece of paper.

3. Have each student illustrate the sentence and share it with their partner.

4. If students are capable of sentence combining, you may ask them to take two of the sentences you wrote, combine them, and illustrate the new sentence.

Family Connections

1. Have students make "snowballs" by crumpling up a piece of paper.

2. Let each student take a "snowball" home.

3. Ask students to use their "snowball" like the Koosh ball in class, throwing it to family members and creating sentences based on a sentence stem. Some sentence stem ideas could be: I like you because . . .; My family is important to me because . . .; or I like to help. . . .

Growing Sentence Stems

Language on a Roll

Activity Overview

Language on a Roll develops a student's ability to enhance and elaborate sentences. Students move from the use of short, truncated sentences to longer, more complex and descriptive sentences.

The Language on a Roll activity engages and motivates students to get excited about building longer sentences through the process of rolling dice. Students create sentences that have at least the same number of words as there are dots on the dice they roll.

Materials

- Pictures to act as prompts
- Dice
- Language on a Roll Worksheet (see Appendix A)

Link to Literacy

Language on a Roll develops students' ability to create more complex sentences in response to a prompt. Students' ability to comprehend longer sentences in text is related to their ability to use longer and more complex sentences orally. The complexity of language that students hear regularly, and can create on their own orally, impacts the complexity of the material they can read, comprehend, and produce in their writing.

Whole-Class Activity

Set the purpose. Say: "You are going to be practicing making longer sentences. When you can speak in longer sentences yourself, you will understand longer sentences when you are listening and reading. And, you will also become better at using longer sentences when you write."

1. Model the activity by first showing the whole group a picture prompt, for example a fancy, fairy-tale carriage. Then, roll the dice and count the number of dots on the side that faces up, once it lands. Create a sentence that relates to the picture and at least the same number of words as the dots you rolled on the dice. For example, if you rolled a 6, maybe create the sentence: *The princess rode in a carriage.*

2. Ask the students if anyone else can come up with a sentence with the same number of words as dots on the dice. (*Cinderella rode in a pretty carriage.*)

3. Roll the dice again until you come up with a larger number than the first roll (this will force students to continue to create longer sentences). Call on a student to create the next

sentence based on the number of dots rolled and the previous sentence. For example, if you rolled a 12, maybe the student would create the sentence: *The princess rode all the way to the palace in a carriage.*

4. Choose another picture, roll the dice, and call on a student to make the first sentence based on that roll. The second roll can be taken by itself if it is higher than the first or it can be added to the first roll (e.g., if the first roll is a 6 and the second is a 4, then the second sentence should be 10 words).

Return to the purpose. Say: "You have been creating bigger sentences. This practice will help you to be better speakers, readers, and writers.

Independent/Paired Activity

1. Have students work with partners.

2. Give students pictures to act as prompts, a pair of dice, and a Language on a Roll Worksheet.

3. Ask partners to take turns. One student is in charge of rolling the dice and the other is the one who creates the sentences.

4. Have one student in each pair roll the dice, count the number of dots, and create a sentence with the same number of words. Have them base the sentence on one of the pictures you provided at the beginning of the activity. For example, if the picture was of an umbrella, the student might do the following based on their roll:

    ☺ Roll of 4 = *I use an umbrella.*
    ☺ Roll of 5 = *An umbrella keeps you dry.*
    ☺ Roll of 6 = *Umbrellas are good in the rain.*

5. Modify the exercise for students who are second-language learners by having them roll only one die for their sentence.

6. Ask students to fill out the Language on a Roll Worksheet with each turn, putting down the number of dots and, beneath it, the sentence they created.

Family Connections

1. Have students take dice and picture prompts home to do this activity with family members.

2. Ask them to create sentences, write them down, and choose three of them to bring back to school.

Language on a Roll

Sentence Ball Toss

Activity Overview

Sentence Ball Toss develops a student's ability to enhance and elaborate sentences. The activity engages students and encourages them to go from using short, truncated sentences to longer, more complex and descriptive sentences. In addition, because the activity is done orally, it enhances purposeful listening and talking. In Sentence Ball Toss students create sentences designed specifically for their oral language level as they toss a Koosh ball back and forth.

Materials

- Koosh ball
- Sentence Ball Toss Picture Worksheet (see Appendix A)

Link to Literacy

Sentence Ball Toss develops students' ability to create more complex sentences in response to a prompt. Students' ability to comprehend longer sentences in text is related to their ability to use longer and more complex sentences orally. The complexity of language that students' hear regularly, and can create on their own orally, impacts the complexity of the material they can read and the level of elaboration they use when they write.

Whole-Class Activity:

Set the purpose. Say: "When you can speak in longer sentences, it helps you to understand longer sentences when you listen and read. It will also help you create more interesting sentences when you write. We are going to build bigger sentences together!"

1. Use a Koosh ball for student engagement and attention.

2. Ask students to stand in a circle. This can be done with a smaller group or a whole class group. It can also be done with students seated and by rolling the Koosh ball.

3. **Sentence Repetition**: This approach encourages active listening. Throw the ball and ask the recipient to repeat the sentence. The student says a simple sentence, the whole group repeats the sentence, and then he throws the ball to someone else and that person repeats the sentence by himself and repeats the activity.

4. **Simple Sentence Expansion**: This is very similar in that it reinforces active listening, but in addition, it begins the process of increasing sentence complexity and language expansion. Say a simple sentence and have the group repeat the sentence. Then toss the ball to a student and encourage the student to create a longer sentence based around the stem you created. A few examples:

   ◦ *"I like to go to the park."*

- ☺ *"I like to go to the park with my family."*
- ☺ *"I like to go to the park and swing on the swings."*
- ☺ *"I like to go to the park and go down the slide."*

Give students the opportunity to listen to the sentence, repeat it, and then add to it. Questions that are open-ended are also good to use for this activity. A few examples:

- ☺ *"How can you help a friend?"*
- ☺ *"I can help a friend by telling the teacher he is hurt."*
- ☺ *"I can help a friend by bringing him his homework if he is sick."*
- ☺ *"I can help a friend by sharing my lunch when he forgets to bring his lunch."*

5. **Structure Syntax**: Another way that this can be done is to structure the use of particular grammatical constructions. For example, students would be asked to add an adjective, an adverb, a conjunction, etc. This is not direct instruction of those concepts but rather an opportunity for students to practice using those concepts orally in sentences.

- ☺ *"I like to read."*
- ☺ *"I like to read about animals."*
- ☺ *"I like to read about places that are far away."*

Some other examples of how this can be used:

- ☺ Teacher and class: *"Michael ran."*
- ☺ (T) *"What else did Michael do?"*
- ☺ (S) *"Michael ran and hid."*
- ☺ (T) *"Where did Michael hide?"*
- ☺ (S) *"Michael ran and hid behind the couch."*

Independent /Paired Activity

1. Decide as a group on one of the most elaborate sentences that was created by the group.

2. Write the sentence on the front board or on chart paper.

3. Students go to their seats and, using their Sentence Ball Toss Picture Worksheet, create a picture of what they visualized when they heard and repeated that sentence.

4. Students copy the sentence under their picture.

Family Connections

(See Family Connections in the Growing Sentence Stems activity.)

1. Students will make "snowballs" by crumpling up a piece of paper.

2. Each student will take a "snowball" home.

3. Students will throw the "snowball" to family members and create sentences based on a sentence stem.

4. Some sentence stem ideas are:
   - ☺ I like you because. . . .
   - ☺ My family is important to me because. . . .
   - ☺ I like to help . . . .

5. Add other sentence stems that relate to your class' interests, areas of study, or need.

Sentence Ball Toss

Word Family Sentences

Activity Overview

Word Family Sentences develops students' ability to flexibly play with language and have fun creating sentences. This activity uses word families as a way to structure sentence creation. Students will choose two or more words from a word family and create a sentence that they will share orally first, then write and illustrate.

Link to Literacy

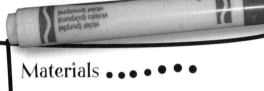

Materials ● ● ● ● ● ● ●

- ◎ Word Family Sentences Worksheet (see Appendix A)
- ◎ Writing paper
- ◎ Word Family List (see Appendix B)
- ◎ Index cards with a variety of word family words written on them
- ◎ Colored markers

Word family learning is a part of literacy development. It supports early decoding skills as students build literacy skills. Word families help students recognize recurring orthographic patterns in words. The study of word families also enhances students' ability to hear and produce rhymes. This activity clearly connects what students are working on and practicing in their reading class to their developing oral language skills.

Whole-Class Activity

Set the purpose. Say: "We are going to play with language and create fun sentences that use some of the words we have learned to read. Learning to play with words helps us speak, read, and write more easily."

1. Put word family words plus words necessary to create sentences (e.g., **had**, **and**, **a**) on index cards or cardstock.

2. Write the following word family words on the front board:
   man – can – fan – Dan – van – ban – Stan
   fat – cat – bat – mat – sat – hat – Pat

3. As a group, choose one word family and read some of the words orally.

4. Create a sentence with the group, for example: *Stan and Dan had a van.*

5. Write the sentence on the front board

6. Expand the sentence with the group, for example: *Stan and Dan had a van with a big fan on the top.*

7. Distribute word family cards to students and ask them to come to the front of the room and create the sentence with their bodies.

8. Illustrate the sentence on the board for the class.

9. Repeat this activity using another sentence, for example: *Dan can fan Stan*. Or, you can repeat the activity with the another word family, making one small sentence, and then a second expanded version with the class. For example:

   fat – cat – bat – mat – sat – hat – Pat

   ☺ *The cat was fat.*

   ☺ *The fat cat named Pat sat on the mat.*

Independent/Paired Activity

1. Have students work in pairs.

2. Give each pair a Word Family List (or a group of index cards with word family words on them) and a Word Family Sentences Worksheet.

3. Ask students to sort the word family cards into the appropriate word families.

4. Let student pairs choose which word family they want to work with as they build sentences.

5. Have them repeat the steps from the whole-class activity:

   ☺ Create a sentence orally (partners can work together on one sentence or they can each create their own sentence).

   ☺ Use the Word Family Sentences Worksheet and write some word family words at the top.

   ☺ Write the sentences on the lines provided on the worksheet.

   ☺ Illustrate the sentence in the drawing box on the worksheet (each partner draws an illustration that matches his or her sentence).

Family Connections

1. To support the use of word families, have students bring home a rhyming book to either read to a family member, have a family member read to them, or read together with their family member.

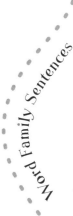

Word Family Sentences

Grammar-Go-Round Sentence Building

Activity Overview

Grammar Go-Round Sentence Building gives students an opportunity to become sentence architects! They'll learn about the building blocks of sentences and use those building blocks to form sentences to share with others. This activity will give students practice with various grammatical constructions, and help them to understand the role of basic sentence building blocks like nouns, verbs, adjectives, and adverbs. In addition, this activity gives students opportunities to create complex and compound sentences. This exposure and practice helps students become more familiar with different sentence constructions in order to understand them as they listen and read.

Materials

- Pictures used to stimulate sentence building
- Grammar-Go-Round Sentence Building Worksheet A (see Appendix A)
- Grammar-Go-Round Sentence Building Worksheet B (see Appendix A)

Link to Literacy

Grammar-Go-Round deepens students' understanding of sentence structure. Comprehension of text is impacted by students' ability to understand various sentence constructions. Often students are used to listening to and speaking in simple sentences. Therefore, a compound sentence or an embedded clause can confuse them and lower their comprehension. Grammar-Go-Round gives students more familiarity with, and understanding of, grammar so that when they encounter such sentences in text, or while listening, they will be better able to make sense of the meaning. In addition, it helps them as they learn to speak in more elaborate and expressive sentences.

Whole-Class Activity

Set the purpose. Say: "You are going to become sentence builders today. By practicing how to build good sentences it will be easier to understand sentences when you are listening and reading. It will also help you to speak and express yourself well."

This activity is designed to be done as a reinforcement of direct grammar instruction that was taught previously.

1. Copy the Grammar-Go-Round Sentence Building Worksheet A onto the front board or create a copy or an overhead transparency to use multiple times on an overhead projector.

2. Write a simple sentence on the front board. (*The children ride bikes.*)

3. Ask the students if they can tell you who the sentence is about. (The sentence is about *the children.*)

4. Fill in the noun circle on the worksheet with the words **the children**.

5. Ask students to tell you what the children do. (*The children ride bikes.*)

6. Fill in the verb circle on the worksheet with the words **ride bikes**.

7. Ask the class if they can tell you something more about the children so that everyone has a better picture of them. A student might suggest, "The children are big." Fill in the adjective circle on the worksheet with the word **big**.

8. Next, ask the class if they can tell you something more about how the children are riding their bikes. (*The children ride carefully.*)

9. Fill in the adverb circle on the worksheet with the word **carefully**.

10. Rewrite the sentence, including the students' suggestions: *The big children ride bikes carefully.*

11. You can ask the students to generate additional ideas about why the children might be riding their bikes carefully.

12. Model the more advanced worksheet (Grammar-Go-Round Sentence Building Worksheet B) by following this procedure:

    ↺ Ask students if they can add to the sentence by thinking about where the children might be going on their bikes. (*The big children ride bikes to the park.*)

    ↺ Next, ask the students why the big children are riding their bikes to the park. (*The big children ride bikes to the park because they want to play.*)

    ↺ Next, ask the students if they can ask a question about the big children that you answer, such as: "How old are the big children?" (*The big children are all twelve years old.*)

    ↺ Next, at the oral practice level, encourage students to think about the question and have them ask another question, such as: "Are the big children all boys or are they a group of boys and girls?"

13. This activity can also be done at a more advanced level by giving direct practice using the words **subject** and **predicate**, and by practicing the creation of compound subjects and compound predicates with conjunctions.

Return to the purpose. Say: "Good sentence builders become better speakers, readers, and writers."

Independent/Paired Activity

1. Give each pair of students a picture that can be used for a sentence prompt and a Grammar-Go-Round Sentence Building Worksheet A to fill out as they create their sentence.

2. This activity can be scaffolded by giving each student a beginning sentence to work with if needed.

Grammar-Go-Round Sentence Building

Family Connections

1. Have students create sentences about their families to share with their families. For example: *My brother plays football. My big brother plays football with his friends.*

2. If appropriate, ask students to use Grammar-Go-Round Sentence Building Worksheet B to create even more elaborate sentences about their family.

Joining Questions and Answers

Activity Overview

Joining Questions and Answers encourages students to answer questions with complete sentences. This activity offers various scaffolds that encourage different ways for students to learn to structure sentences. In the same way that we teach students to read a question and restate the question as they formulate a written response, this activity encourages oral practice using this effective strategy.

What you talk about matters. Choose relevant topics with useful vocabulary. The activity is built around content-area topics, or topics taken from text reading. The teacher starts with a question about the topic and students are asked to include part of the teacher's question in their responses. It is very simple, but effectively helps students develop oral responses that are more deeply connected to the original question.

> ## Materials
>
> - Topics based on relevant content-area material or stories that have been read to the group
> - Passages with questions for partner reading
> - White boards
> - Dry-erase markers

Link to Literacy

Joining Questions and Answers teaches students to make meaningful connections as they respond to focused questions, both orally and in text. Older students are often taught this for written responses, but it can be equally effective at the oral level for students of all ages and can be transferred to written responses after it is practiced orally.

Whole-Class Activity

Set the purpose. Say: "Learning to listen to questions carefully is important. You will be practicing careful listening and then will learn how to build your answer so that it connects to the question."

1. Choose a topic that is relevant to your own curriculum and in which you have confidence that you have developed enough background knowledge.

   The following is a sample passage from *The Six-Minute Solution: A Reading Fluency Program*, by G. Adams and S. Brown, 2007, Longmont, CO: Sopris West Educational Services.

The Hopi: Native Americans of the Southwest

Many hundreds of years ago, the Hopi lived in what is now Arizona. These Native Americans were desert people. They lived on top of steep hills with flat tops. These hills are called mesas. The Hopi built their houses out of rocks covered with a plaster. The plaster was made of clay and water. Then they joined

their houses into villages. The Hopi villages are called pueblos. When a Hopi man and woman married, they lived in the woman's house. Hopi women owned the houses in the pueblo. The Hopi men had a special room that was underground. This room is called a kiva. The Hopi men gathered in the kiva for special meetings. Women were only allowed in the kiva on special occasions.

2. Create a series of questions that are generated from the specific learning students may have done in your class. For example, for the preceding passage, ask students the following question (write it on the front board): "Where did the Hopi live?" Prompt your students to answer using part of the question. Model the first answer: "The Hopi lived in Arizona."

3. Write the answer on the board and underline the part of the question and the part of the answer that match. You might use the same color marker to underline the matching parts.

4. Ask the students another question: "What kind of houses did the Hopi live in?" (The Hopi lived in houses that were made of rocks covered with plaster.)

5. Repeat this activity with several questions at the oral level.

6. Then, repeat the activity and extend it to the written level. Ask the question orally and write it on the front board. (Students will listen to the oral question and read the question on the board to remember the wording and check spelling.)

7. Have students formulate their answers on individual white boards, underlining the part of their response that matches the part they used from your oral question.

8. Explain to students that this practice is called restating a question to form an answer.

Independent/Paired Activity

1. Give students a passage with questions written underneath.

2. Have students pair up, read the passage with their partner, and then read the questions orally.

3. Ask students to take turns answering the questions orally, using the restating strategy they learned and practiced in the group activity.

4. When students have practiced at the oral level, have them begin writing the answers to the questions. Be sure to check their responses and remind them to underline the parts of the question and the responses they've created that match.

Family Connections

1. Ask students to practice asking a family member questions. Have them teach the family member to restate the question as they answer it. For example:
   ↺ Student: "What is your favorite food?"
   ↺ Family member: "Pizza."
   ↺ Student guides family member to restate the question in the answer.
   ↺ Family member: "My favorite food is pizza."

2. Generate a list of family questions with your class so the students who need more structure will be able to use the questions the class generated at home.

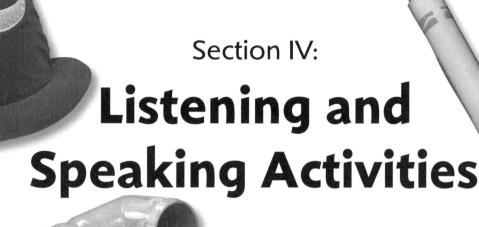

Section IV:
Listening and Speaking Activities

The activities in this section are designed to give students the opportunity to practice speaking and listening actively within a small group or as a member of a larger group. Giving students the opportunity to engage in stimulating discussions and share their knowledge orally in the classroom on a daily basis will help them apply the words and concepts that have been studied in both oral and written expression. Speaking both reflects a person's thinking and furthers his or her thinking. When you give students more words and concepts to think about, you can facilitate their ability to engage in more effective communication orally and in writing. Students will use their words in purposeful activities that help them to share and apply their knowledge. While growing vocabulary is important, it is most effective when the words are used and shared in meaningful activities. In addition, students will practice listening to each other and develop a deeper understanding that listening is as active as speaking when one is engaged in the process of learning and sharing.

Be the Storyteller

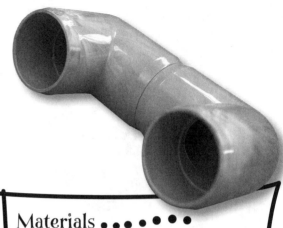

Activity Overview

Be the Storyteller is an activity that gets students actively involved in speaking as they use props and a microphone to tell a story to the other students in the class. The story could be real or imaginary. This activity builds background knowledge and moves it beyond simply dispensing knowledge to something accessible, vital, and exciting for the students.

This activity can be used to enhance content area learning. The use of pictures and props to introduce the Boston Tea Party, life in Colonial America, a wagon train journey, or being a firefighter, stimulates the students' imaginations and helps them develop a mental model. This activity increases engagement so that students are more willing and able to listen attentively and speak enthusiastically.

Materials

- Access to materials for research
- Tape recorders and whisper-phones
- Microphone (real or play)
- Props, costumes
- Chart paper and assorted stickers

Link to Literacy

Be the Storyteller supports literacy as students listen, watch, and/or read to gather information about the time, place, and period they are studying. Students list new and interesting words important to their story topic, collect and draw pictures, and summarize information through conversation and presentations. The orally shared stories enhance the whole class's information base as they listen and learn. Students will also write their narratives, transferring what they have learned from the oral level to the written level.

Whole-Class Activity

Set the purpose. Say: "We are going to tell and act out stories for each other. Since we will be telling different stories we will learn about a lot of different things."

The preparation for this activity can be done over the course of several days. The activity should be tied to topics that have authenticity to your class studies and interests. Model for your class:

1. Choose a topic and tell the class what you did to research that topic. Bring in some of the resources you used, read a book, or even show a short video about the topic.

2. Ask some students to help you or use a few props to help bring your story to life. Be sure to modulate your voice and use gestures as you tell your story.

3. Give your students a list of possible topics they might want to use to create their own story.

4. Tell students they may work individually or in small groups. You will probably want to assign the groups (carefully choosing students who will work well together and students who balance each other in terms of shyness and comfort in public speaking, reading, and writing skills). Encourage shy students to work in groups and be sure to differentiate their roles, so the shy student can participate in a way in which he or she is comfortable, yet still stretched in terms of oral language skills.

Return to the purpose. Say: "You have all been telling wonderful stories and have learned from each other."

Independent/Paired Activity

During presentations you may want to prepare a chart on card stock or graph paper called "What We Have Learned." List all the topics students discussed and leave some space for stickers to be placed next to the individual topics. The stickers will represent details and concepts recalled by the listeners.

1. Let students choose the topic they are interested in. Go over the Write and Speak About list below:

   Write and Speak About
   - Topics or people you have seen in videos, movies, or on TV (superheroes, historical characters, or real heroes)
   - Subjects you are studying (for example, American Colonists or Native Americans)
   - A story you have heard or read
   - Personal subjects (pets, family, vacations, or hobbies)

2. Give students access to various forms of research (books, Internet, videos, field trips).

3. Have students do this activity over time, so they can research, study, take notes, write and prepare speeches, and perform demonstrations to share with the class. Remind them to follow these steps, in order, before presenting:
   - Illustrate your stories
   - Practice your story aloud
   - Use expression (change your voice to express fear, excitement, happiness, etc.)
   - Use gesture
   - Use costumes and props
   - Read the story to a small group or to the class if that makes you more comfortable
   - Tell the story if you know it well enough

4. Have students present when they are finally ready to share their story with others.

5. Give them a microphone if they want it.

6. Let students use props, pictures, music, or whatever is necessary to make their speeches interactive, engaging, and meaningful to themselves and the class.

Be the Storyteller

7. Ask the class to use their active listening skills as they listen to the student or students who are speaking. They may take notes during the course of the presentation. They will be asked to recall information from the presentation when it is over.

8. The students who are listening should also think of questions they might want to ask the presenters and write them down.

9. After the presentation is over, give listening students an opportunity to ask questions of the presenters.

10. Ask students to volunteer what they remember from the presentation.

11. Place a sticker (little stars or hearts work well) on the "What We Have Learned" chart each time students offer a detail that show they were listening actively. You might add up all the stickers for a topic and say, "You listened so well that you remember 12 details about (whatever the topic was)."

Family Connections

1. Have students practice and present their stories at home before giving them in class.

2. Give students stickers to take home and present to their family members as incentive for them to recall as many details as they can about the students' stories. Have students place the stickers on a homework note with this assignment. The note should be returned to school with the stickers on it.

Carousel of Knowledge

Activity Overview

The Carousel of Knowledge emphasizes the important role that knowledge plays in building literacy. When students are given the opportunity to share the knowledge they have learned they begin to feel more capable as learners and their self-esteem and motivation build. One of the important goals in this activity is to raise the level of knowledge for the entire class. The teacher will divide the class, giving each group a different topic of study, and then, once the different groups have researched their topics, students will share what they have learned with the rest of the class. This builds a classroom climate where students take pride in becoming teachers for each other. It provides students with a chance to enhance their cultural background knowledge with more information than they could have gathered alone.

The Carousel of Knowledge involves students in research and study on topics either selected by the teacher or the class, depending on the situation. For example, if the class is doing a hero study, small groups may be assigned (or may choose) a particular hero to study. They will read, discuss, and use the Internet to find information about the person they are studying. Then they will teach what they have learned in an engaging manner to the class.

Materials

- Books, films, pictures, articles, Internet sites that relate to the topic of study
- Carousel of Knowledge Planning Guide (see Appendix A)
- Carousel of Knowledge Planning Wheel (see Appendix A)
- Tips for Creating Engagement (see Appendix B)

Link to Literacy

The Carousel of Knowledge focuses on the development of background knowledge. This knowledge supports reading comprehension by helping students create a mental model that can be applied to new learning. This enhanced background knowledge adds to the deposits students have in their "background knowledge bank" and can be drawn upon for listening and reading comprehension. It also helps students become more informed speakers and writers.

Whole-Class Activity

Set the purpose. Say: "This activity will give you the chance to learn a lot about a topic, figure out fun and engaging ways to share that knowledge, and be a teacher!"

1. Model this activity by introducing a general topic to the class, for example, hero study, colonists in early America, the Westward Expansion, or a geology unit. This can be done at a simple level (a particular animal's habitat in the first grade, or at a more complex level for older students—for example, causes of the Civil War).

Carousel of Knowledge

2. Give students enough general information on the topic to pique their interest, but try to leave them wanting more. For example, if their topic is hero study, brainstorm with them, discuss, and watch a video about the hero to build interest and act as a teaser. Let them know that when everyone is finished with their research there will be many opportunities to learn new things about each of the people they are studying.

3. Use picture books to build visual concepts about the topic.

4. Divide the students up as "individual researchers" or form them into "research teams." It is best to decide this for students based on their reading skills coupled with their ability to work independently.

5. Assign research topics with careful groupings.

Independent/Paired Activity

1. Have students work independently in their groups choosing books, reading, researching, and, finally, sharing information about their assigned topic with the other students in the group.

2. You may assign more capable students to take notes and share their notes with the students who need more scaffolding.

3. Distribute the Carousel of Knowledge Planning Guide and Wheel to all students individually in their groups. Depending on the level of the students, you can fill out part of the Planning Guide ahead of time, leaving some information for the students to gather themselves, but allowing them to follow the example you have modeled for them in the first part of the notes.

4. After students have completed and shared their Planning Guide answers within their group, have them check their answers with you. The Carousel of Knowledge Planning Wheel is a tool that can be used in conjunction with the Planning Guide. It is helpful for more visual learners and gives students a broader view of the topic before they delve into the details.

5. After you have checked students' planning tools, let them plan their presentation. This can take the form of a report, play, song, multi-sensory exhibit with written explanation, etc.

6. Plan time for the student groups to share their research-based presentations with the rest of the class.

7. Encourage active listening by asking the class to create questions for the presenters.

Family Connections

1. Have students practice their presentations at home.

2. Invite families to school for the presentations.

Word Catchers

Activity Overview

Word Catchers emphasizes the concept that speaking and listening both take attention and engagement. It gives students the opportunity to think about and practice listening with engagement while they experience it as an active part of communication. Through this activity, students concentrate on listening by holding a butterfly net and "catching" the words of the speaker. After the speaker is finished, the listener must retell or summarize what the speaker said to him or her. The net, therefore, becomes a symbol of students' ability to capture and recall what someone has told them.

Materials •••••••

- Butterfly nets (bought or made with a dowel and tulle fabric)
- Toy microphone
- Paper and pencils

Link to Literacy

Oral language helps to provide the foundation for reading comprehension and written language. When students engage in activities that enhance attention and listening, and then practice retelling or summarization, it gives them meaningful practice so they can become better at both reading and writing responses to what was read.

Whole-Class Activity

Set the purpose. Say: "This activity will help you learn that when people talk to each other the speaker is not the only one who has to pay attention. When we listen carefully we learn more. We will be practicing a fun way to pay attention to our Talking Buddy."

1. Make one student the official "word catcher" for the group. The student is given the butterfly net and "catches" the words the speaker speaks.

2. Make one student the first speaker. He or she can be given a prop, such as a toy microphone. The speaker may speak about something that is related to a vocabulary word you are studying or content from your class study. It could also be about a personal experience.

3. Tell the other students who are listening that they should also "catch" the words of the speaker and turn them into pictures in their minds.

4. When the speaker is through, give the word catcher with the butterfly net an opportunity to retell or summarize what the speaker said.

5. Give other student catchers in the group the opportunity to add details or make corrections to the retell or summary of the word catcher. For example, if the speaker was describing his pet dog, the word catcher may retell some details about the dog's color and size. However, the rest of the class may remember additional points they heard about the pet being fun to play ball with and to walk.

6. Give the speaker an opportunity to respond and make additions or corrections.

7. This activity can be repeated with another speaker and another word catcher.

Return to the purpose. Say: "Learning to be a word catcher will help you to learn and remember more when you are listening and reading."

Independent/Paired Activity

1. Have students choose, or assign them to, their Talking Buddy.

2. Ask students to choose who will be the first speaker and who will be the first listener or "word catcher" in each pair.

3. Give the listener a butterfly net. Remind the listener that as he or she catches the words, he or she should try to turn them into pictures.

4. The speaker can also be given a prop, such as a toy microphone.

5. After the speaker is done, have the listener ask questions to fill in details or make corrections to his or her mental image of the speaker's topic.

6. Have the listener retell or summarize what the speaker said to him or her. Ask the speaker to add or correct the retell. (Some students may be able to go to their desks and create a written retell based on listening to their partners.)

7. Ask the partners to switch roles and repeat the activity.

Family Connections

1. Have students take turns borrowing the butterfly nets to bring home.

2. During conversations with family members, ask students to take turns with their family members "catching," and then retelling or summarizing each other's words.

Getting to Know My Family

Activity Overview

Getting to Know My Family gives students a framework for talking to family members and structures positive communication between students and their parents. In addition, students gain specific knowledge about their family which they can, in turn, share with classmates.

Link to Literacy

Getting to Know My Family encourages student-parent talk in the home. This is critical to developing oral language, the foundation of reading comprehension. In addition, the simple, yet structured, nature of this activity encourages positive interactions, enhancing students' confidence in themselves as learners.

Materials

- Photos or drawings of family members
- Getting to Know My Family Worksheet (see Appendix A)
- Tape recorder
- Instant white boards or note paper
- Drawing paper
- Markers
- Camera
- Invitation to family members to come to the classroom when their student is presenting
- Props (hats, outfits, books, or tools) to enhance understanding about the chosen family member

Whole-Class Activity

Set the purpose. Say: "You are going to decide which member of your family you want to learn more about. Then, you will gather information about that family member and share it with the class."

1. Model for students by describing a family member of your own. Have a picture of that person, perhaps a "prop" that is special to that person (such as a favorite book) and fill out the Getting to Know My Family Worksheet in front of the class.

2. Ask the class to visualize the person you are describing. Make your description as colorful and in-depth as possible. You might even want to place a photo or drawing in the middle of the board and then add words around the photo that describe your family member, such as kind, funny, giving, smart, loves reading, loves skiing, and can play the piano.

3. Once you are done presenting, ask the class to recall as many details about your family member as they can. Put a checkmark or star on the board for each detail the students can remember.

Getting to Know My Family

Return to the purpose. Say: "Learning to listen and remember will help you to be better readers. It is fun to learn more about the people we care about."

Independent/Paired Activity I

1. Ask students to choose a family member in class and then take home their Getting to Know My Family Worksheet.

2. If necessary, the students may take a class camera home to take a picture of their relative, or they can draw a picture or bring in a photo from home.

3. Ask students to interview their chosen family member using the Getting to Know My Family Worksheet, and to bring in a photo or picture of him or her.

4. Have them create a poster similar to your example on the board with the family member's picture in the middle surrounded by several words that describe him or her. (The words can be written in different color markers.)

5. Have students put the words from the poster together to create a paragraph or essay (depending on age level) about their family member.

Independent/Paired Activity II

1. Have students plan how they will present the information about their family member to the whole class by sharing ideas in a small group.

2. When ready to present to the whole class, have students use props, their poster, or ask them to read their paragraph or essay.

3. Ask the other members of the class to take notes on a white board or paper for each student's presentation, noting the key words and details they believe really paint a picture of the family member being discussed.

4. Ask the class to remember ten details they learned from the student presenting about his or her family member.

5. Assign one student to make a checkmark, or place a sticker, on the "What We Have Learned" chart (used previously in the Be the Storyteller activity) for each detail recalled by the participants. This will acknowledge the class's active listening and encourage students who have been speaking.

Family Connections

1. Invite the family in to participate or listen to the report on the family member highlighted. (Send them a formal invitation a week or so before their student is supposed to present.)

2. Invite the family member to tell a story or tell something extra about themselves to the class.

3. Invite the family member to make a check mark or place a sticker on the board for each detail recalled about him or her.

Reflections on My Learning

Worksheet 18

Reflections on My Learn

1. What is your favorite part of today's lesson?
   My favorite part of today's lesson is _____

2. What part of the lesson connects to something you alrea
   I already knew about _____ and I conn
   learned today about _____

3. What was the most interesting new thing you learned
   The most interesting new thing that I learned today is
   _____

4. What is something you would like to learn more ab
   I want to learn more about _____

5. Was there any part of the lesson today that confus
   The part of the lesson that confused me was _____

Activity Overview

Reflections on My Learning gives students the opportunity to reflect on their daily learning. It is based on the concept that learning is deepened by the reflection that occurs after learning. Having students articulate what they learn each day reinforces daily learning and enhances retention. Through a series of questions students are guided toward insights about the day's lesson and its connection to previous learning.

Link to Literacy

One of the fundamental lynchpins of learning is the ability to attach old learning to new learning. This process of connection helps students place the new learning within a context that acts as a hook for recall, retrieval, and application. This important cognitive process supports comprehension in listening, reading, and all learning situations. Students with weak background knowledge are at a disadvantage that will affect future learning. Reflections on My Learning requires reflection and connection at a conscious level and can have a positive impact on a student's ability to learn.

Materials • • • • • • •

- Reflections on My Learning Worksheet (see Appendix A)
- Reflections on My Learning Venn Diagram (see Appendix A)
- Knowledge Notebook (a 1-inch, 3-ring binder to hold students' Reflections on My Learning Worksheets and other materials)
- 3-hole punched plastic sheet protectors

Whole-Class Activity

Set the purpose. Say: "It is easier to learn things when you have some piece of information that you already know about the subject you are studying. Then you can attach what you already know to the new information you are learning. You are going to think about what you already know and what you are currently learning about. Then you will think about how you use the old knowledge to help deepen your understanding of the new knowledge."

1. Draw the Reflections on My Learning Venn Diagram on the front board.

2. Introduce the new learning, for example: "We will be learning about some causes of the American Revolution." "We will be learning about the three states of matter." "We will be learning about the challenges faced by the early American colonists."

3. Give students an overview of the topic, read a book about it, clarify terms, and show objects and pictures as you build background knowledge that is meaningful and contextualized.

Reflections on My Learning

4. Ask students to give their ideas about what they've learned in the past (this past learning could be from a lesson you taught yesterday) that relates to the overview of what they are about to learn.

5. Fill in the "What I Knew" circle of the Venn Diagram with some of the information students generate about past learning.

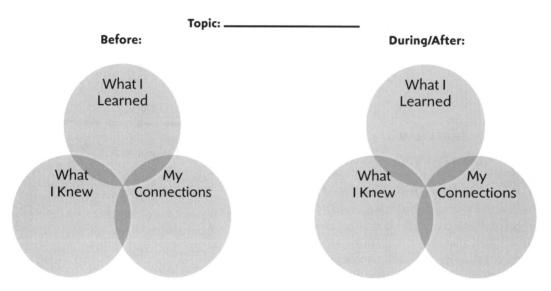

Topic: _____

Before:

What I Learned

What I Knew

My Connections

During/After:

What I Learned

What I Knew

My Connections

6. Teach the full lesson and return to the Venn Diagram at the end.

7. Ask for students to state what they remember about what they just learned.

8. Fill in the "What I Learned" circle of the Venn Diagram.

9. Ask the students to think about how they used their old knowledge to help them understand the new learning.

10. Fill in the "My Connections" circle in the Venn Diagram. For example, based on the previous topic of the American Colonists, students might say: "The early American colonists did not have enough food to eat. My Brownie Troop collected cans of food for people who do not have enough food to eat in our town."

11. Summarize what the class knew, what they learned, and some of the connections the students used to help learn and remember the new learning.

12. Eventually you may ask students to do the summarization process by themselves.

Return to the purpose. Say: "You can learn more and remember it more easily when you think about connecting what you are learning to things you have already learned about or done in your life."

Independent/Paired Activity

1. Give each student a Reflections on My Learning Venn Diagram, a Reflections on My Learning Worksheet, a plastic sheet protector, and a Knowledge Notebook.

2. Ask students to work with a partner and talk about what they have learned about the chosen topic for the activity.

3. Have them work together and fill in their diagrams.

4. Ask students to use their completed diagrams to help them remember the information they need to complete their Reflections on My Learning Worksheet.

5. Have students place their worksheets in plastic sheet protectors and place them in their Knowledge Notebooks.

Family Connections

1. Have students go home, share their worksheets with their family, and teach and share their new knowledge with them.

2. Make time to share any family responses students bring to class from home.

3. You may choose to ask for parents' signatures on the worksheets to show that they talked about the information with their student.

Reflections on My Learning

The Story Train

Activity Overview

The Story Train uses the framing device of a train with separate cars to assist students in the creation of a narrative retell or original story. Each train car represents an essential piece of the story. For example, one car has the title/theme; the next states who (main character)/what; the third may state where (setting)/when; the next, events/goals; the next, problems; and the final car, solutions.

Materials • • • • • • •

- ❂ Story Train Worksheet (see Appendix A)
- ❂ Index cards to create "story cards/cars" for the "Story Train"
- ❂ 3-hole punched plastic sheet protectors
- ❂ Chart paper for students

Link to Literacy

This activity strengthens students' ability to sequence and structure oral language for storytelling and story retelling. Through practice with external structures, students begin to internalize critical story elements and become better able to later retell or create a story on their own. This skill supports students' comprehension of a story by giving them a deeper understanding of its elements.

Whole-Class Activity

Set the purpose. Say: "If you want to talk about or retell something you have read, it will be easier if you organize the information you want to speak about. Organizing the information will help you to remember it, recall it, and link it to other things you know. When you do this it will make it easier for you to share what you have learned."

Prior to the activity, choose a story your class has been reading or listening to, or a content area theme they have been studying as the subject for modeling the "Story Train." Using the Story Train Worksheet as a model, create index cards with magnetic tape on the back of each so they can be placed on the front board as you build the train.

1. Tell students the theme or story of your Story Train. Place the index cards in a linear fashion on the board to represent the cars of a train. For example, if you are going to be working on the book, *Little House on the Prairie* by Laura Ingalls Wilder, then write the title and author on the first card. (If you are working on a unit of study, such as service learning, the first card might say "helping others.")

2. Next, write the following on the remaining cards:
   - ↺ 2nd card: Who/What = Laura, quick sketch, character descriptors (e.g., brave, funny).
   - ↺ 3rd card: Where/Setting = Little house in Kansas.
   - ↺ 4th card: Events/Goals = A sentence and pictures (e.g., "Laura's family moved to Kansas").

○ 5th card: Problem = A sentence and pictures (e.g., "Laura walked past a rattlesnake").

○ 6th card: Solution = A sentence and pictures (e.g., "Laura saved her dog").

3. When you have a number of cards on the board, draw details around the cars that make them look like a train. For example, draw a smokestack and smoke coming out of the first car and wheels on all the cars.

4. Ask someone to retell what you have created by looking at the train. For example: "Laura is brave, funny, and kind. I know she is brave because I remember when she saved her dog. I know she is funny because she loved to learn to spit with Mr. Edwards. I know she is kind because even though she is young, she cares about others." The sentences that you generated as you were building the train make the retelling easy because the students can look at the board and go from the name to the detail to the complete sentence.

5. Leave your model up on the front board when you ask students to create their own version of the train (or have them work on a different story).

Independent/Paired Activity

1. Distribute index cards to students. Determine how many cards (or how long you want the Story Train to be) depending on student ability level and what has been directly taught in the past.

2. Have students work in pairs to create one new Story Train.

3. Distribute the Story Train Worksheets and ask student pairs to work together to fill them out (each student gets a worksheet, but they can collaborate on the answer). They will then use the worksheet as the basis for creating a Story Train.

4. Have them work together to create the first two cars of their Story Trains. They can base their trains on the current story they are reading or a thematic unit you are studying as a class. For some students, it will be appropriate for them to simply copy the work you did on the board. Other students may use the same model and then expand the work you did previously.

5. Have students create the first card/car (title/theme [with author]).

6. Have students create the second card/car (who/what [main character]). Have them write a sentence about the character and draw a picture representing him or her.

7. Ask students to make one connection to their own life based on the content.
For example: "I was once brave when...." Or, "My brother is funny like Laura because he tells jokes and does magic tricks."

8. Ask students to continue adding more cards/cars to their train.

9. After they have completed the train and worksheet, have them share their work orally with the class.

The Story Train

10. Give students a long piece of chart paper to mount their train (have them save the worksheet for the Family Connections activity). Ask them to glue the train to the paper and then decorate the paper to look like a train.

11. Display the Story Trains in the room or hall outside your classroom.

Family Connections

Prior to this activity, have students add a "Story Trains" section to their Knowledge Notebooks (from the Reflections on My Learning activity).

1. Have students put their Story Train Worksheet from the Individual/Paired Activity into a plastic sheet protector to take home to their families.

2. Ask them to retell the story on the worksheet to their family members.

3. Have students return the Story Train Worksheet to school and place it their Knowledge Notebooks. Encouraging students to review their Story Train Worksheets on a regular basis will help them recall past stories that have been read and retold.

Heroic Conversations

Heroes Hall of Fame Certificate

[NAME]

Is hereby inducted in to the Heroes Hall of Fame for his or her work:

Date: _____

Approved by: _____

Activity Overview

Heroic Conversations is an activity that combines valuable cultural learning about heroes with opportunities for listening, speaking, and conversation. In addition, there are structured activities that move learning from the oral language level to the written level. The opportunity to share knowledge enhances the background knowledge of the entire class, while making students more confident about their ability to learn, speak, and teach others.

Link to Literacy

Heroic Conversations builds students' knowledge and helps them deepen their connection to valuable content. Students will study, listen to, read about, and discuss heroic people and their work, then move their learning from text reading to writing. Background knowledge is related to reading comprehension. The more general knowledge students bring with them to the text they are reading, the more likely it will be that they can make meaningful connections to it.

Materials • • • • • • •

- List of Heroes (see Appendix B)
- Heroic Conversations Worksheet (see Appendix A)
- Heroes Hall of Fame Certificate (see Appendix B)
- Books, videos, passages, about a particular hero or heroes
- Self-stick notes
- Index cards
- Speaker's Notebook
- Props for acting out heroic acts or heroes' lives
- Tape recorder

Whole-Class Activity

Set the purpose. Say: "This activity will help you listen, learn, read, speak, and write about someone you think has done something heroic." Prior to the activity, choose a list of potential heroes for your class to study.

1. Briefly read about each of the heroes you've chosen for the class, then tell them that you are choosing one in particular who has impressed you with his or her heroic acts.

2. Model by taking time to teach something about one of the heroes you have chosen through the use of reading, watching a video, and sharing information from Internet research.

3. Let the class get involved and respond to the information, giving them opportunities for engagement and responsive feedback. For example, if you have read a book about Jackie Robinson, a student might remember something he had learned earlier and add it to the conversation (e.g., "Jackie was famous for stealing home" or "Jackie played for the Dodgers and played an important role in ending segregation in Major League Baseball").

Heroic Conversations

4. Dig in further by modeling one or two of the following activities for the students to use later for their own hero study:

   a. Bring in pictures and demonstrate the construction of a hero poster. This can be a collage or it can have the hero's photo in the middle and words, events, or accomplishments that are significant to that person's life radiating out from the photo.

   b. Use a box or bag and put objects in it that signify ideas, places, or events for the hero being described. Have students take turns choosing an object and talking about what they learned about how that object connects to the hero.

   c. Dress up like the hero and give an oral report.

   d. Get a few students together to "be the experts" and create a panel discussion with questions and answers from the student audience. If your students cannot generate enough questions for the panel, give out index cards with questions already on them for them to read and ask.

   e. Get a couple of students together to help you act out an important event in the hero's life.

   f. Create a Select and Connect-type activity where students are asked to connect two words from two lists that are on a piece of paper and talk about how those words are related in terms of the hero.

   g. Scaffold note-taking by providing notes for the class that cover the content presented about the hero being studied. (These notes can be completely filled in and given as a study guide in order to give students a model of good note-taking, or they can be partially filled in and students can fill in the missing pieces.)

   h. Create structured notes about the hero using a "T-note" format, with the main idea and details across the top of the "T," and pictures that create a visual memory of details related to the hero being studied, vertically below.

   i. Share your favorite thing about the hero with your Talking Buddy or another student in the class.

   j. Model writing a good topic sentence about your hero. Ask students to add to or create their own sentence orally. Write some of their suggestions and modifications on the board.

5. Finally, release students to do a hero study of their own.

Return to the purpose. Say: "The more you learn about important people, places, and events, the more knowledge you will have to help you learn more new things."

Independent/Paired Activity

1. Give your own List of Heroes to students or write your list on the board. Give them the Heroic Conversations Worksheet.

2. Have students work in small groups (or individually if they prefer) and choose one of the heroes.

3. Have them complete the Heroic Conversations Worksheet and then choose two or three different ways they will share their study with the entire class. They can use ideas from the model that you provided about your hero study or one that you did not model. Briefly give examples and explanations of additional choices you did not show during the previous whole-class activity.

4. Have students share their work with other students, leaving a poster, box of objects, or notes as "evidence" of the study, which can be put on display in the classroom.

5. Create a "Hero Hall of Fame" where information and pictures of all the students' heroes are mounted. Give each student a Heroes Hall of Fame Certificate and have them fill in the information about their hero before mounting it on the wall.

Family Connections

1. Ask students to tell their family members about the hero they studied in class.

2. Have them ask if the family members know about the hero or have any memories of the person. Have them ask their family members what they think of the hero. (Let students borrow a tape recorder ahead of time to record their family members' thoughts about the hero so the class can hear them.)

3. Have students write a sentence or paragraph that summarizes what their family members believe about the hero. Ask students to share it with the class.

4. Invite family members to class to add to the discussion about the hero if they are able to contribute.

Heroic Conversations

The Conversation Assembly

Activity Overview

The Conversation Assembly demonstrates a schoolwide commitment to oral language. The entire school (or a certain grade level) meets at assembly for a Conversation Assembly. The principal, the kitchen staff, the bus drivers, the coaches, and music teachers can all be invited for a Conversation Assembly about a given topic. They can all come to one assembly or they may stagger and come as guests to various ones.

> ## Materials......
> ⊚ A short video presentation
> ⊚ A poem, dramatization, visual art, music
> ⊚ A short story
> ⊚ A short expository text

The Conversation Assembly will offer opportunities for modeling good language and conversation centered around a particular subject. For example, if it is Thanksgiving, there may be a video or presentation about the meaning of Thanksgiving. If it is time to begin preparing for the Science Fair, the topic could relate to that subject. This activity supports conversation by demonstrating that it is appreciated and valued schoolwide.

Through this activity students build common knowledge about a topic, then watch and listen to models of conversation, and finally engage in conversation with a neighbor. They may also have the opportunity to summarize their conversation for the group.

Link to Literacy

Oral language skills support listening comprehension as well as reading comprehension. Whether reading or listening, students' ability to take in new information, link it to background knowledge, and use that knowledge in a conversation can deepen learning. The Conversation Assembly includes listening, reflecting, questioning, talking, and responding based on knowledge presented during the assembly.

Whole-Class Activity

Set the purpose. Say: "We are going to learn something together and then have an opportunity to talk about what we have learned. Having interesting conversations can help us learn and remember better."

1. Introduce a topic that will be covered in the Conversation Assembly to the class through reading, listening to a speaker, watching a play or a video, or viewing paintings to build background about that topic of conversation. The topic should be relevant to school activities and values, such as areas of common study or service (e.g., preparing for a food collection for a local food pantry).

2. Have students assemble in the usual manner to listen to the principal or a designated teacher introduce the topic. As part of this introduction, this person might choose to read a book, show a video, or share relevant facts.

3. Next, invite two (carefully chosen) people to sit on the stage and begin a discussion about the topic of study. For example, if the topic is a food collection, you could invite the cafeteria manager and the principal to talk about nutrition and how the collection will help members of the local community.

4. Make sure the conversation is transparent about linking background knowledge to what students have just learned.

5. Have the people on the stage ask the audience a few questions about the topic.

6. Have them ask the students in the audience to turn to a neighbor and have a one- to two-minute conversation about the topic.

7. Have them bring the students back to attention and ask for a couple of volunteers to come to the stage, summarize, and share their conversations with the audience.

8. When students return to the classroom, ask them to either draw a picture about what they learned or write a paragraph about it.

9. Give some students, who want to pursue learning on the topic, an opportunity to further their knowledge about the topic. For example, you can have them go to the library or write to an expert in the field. Have them plan to share what they have learned with the entire class.

Family Connections

1. Encourage students to share what they learned at the Conversation Assembly with their families and have a conversation on the topic with them.

The Conversation Assembly

Let the Experts Explain

Activity Overview

Let the Experts Explain emphasizes information gathering and sharing so students can become "experts." When students become "experts" in something it gives them a belief in themselves as learners. Topics of study can vary depending on students' age or the same topic may be covered at different age levels. Students work individually or in small collaborative groups. During group study, students work cooperatively to build background knowledge with the purpose of sharing it with others. The students then either prepare a speech individually or plan on dividing a speech between several group members. There are several kinds of speeches that can be used for this activity: informative, demonstrative, or persuasive.

Materials

- Speech Topics for Students (see Appendix B)
- Microphone
- Props
- Tape recorder
- Chart paper
- Research materials (books, videos, interviews with local experts, etc.)

Link to Literacy

Exploration and research for speech-making involves reading and analyzing, note-taking and the interpretation of notes, and, finally, transcribing notes to create a lively and interesting presentation to share with others. These skills are all directly related to the skills necessary for reading comprehension, writing, and gathering knowledge, and support future comprehension. Choosing a topic of interest increases personal investment, motivation, and attention. Giving students choices between informing, demonstrating, or persuading allows students with different strengths and comfort levels to participate.

Whole-Class Activity

Set the purpose. Say: "We are going to gather information and then share it with each other. Since we will each be gathering different information, we will all gain from each other's knowledge. You will each become an expert on a topic and will share that expertise with others so that they will learn from you."

Prepare for this activity over the course of several days. The activity should be tied to topics that have authenticity to your class's studies and interests. You will be demonstrating three kinds of speeches: informative, demonstrative, and persuasive.

- An "informative" speech shares information gathered about a topic with the goal of teaching the listener new information.

◉ A "demonstrative" speech involves a demonstration of something that has been learned, like how to do something or how to make something.

◉ A "persuasive" speech shares information with the goal of imparting a point of view and persuading the listeners to agree or act in a certain way.

1. Choose a topic and tell the class what you did to research that topic. You might bring in some of the resources you used and even show a short video or read a book or article about the topic.

   Give a short **informative** speech about the topic. Illustrate your speech with pictures and perhaps a costume or simple props.

2. Next, choose a different topic for a **demonstrative** speech. Follow the same procedures as before in terms of discussing your research about the topics to the class. This time, however, model how a demonstrative speech is given. For example, show the class how to decorate a cake, your favorite yoga poses, or how to sign the alphabet.

3. Repeat this activity another day with a third topic. Model a **persuasive** speech for it, such as why we should recycle, recess should be longer because…, I believe kindness can be taught because….

4. Give your students the Speech Topics for Students list with possible topics in each speech category (informative, demonstrative, and persuasive). Have them generate additional ideas. Put these ideas on chart paper at the front of the class so they can be seen in the room and studied by students as they make their decisions about the kind of speech they are going to make.

5. Tell students they may work individually or in small groups. You will assign the groups (carefully choosing students who work well together and students who balance each other in terms of shyness and public speaking comfort). Encourage shy students to work in groups and be sure to differentiate their roles so they can participate in a way in which they are comfortable yet stretched in terms of oral language skills (e.g., they can participate in the research or planning discussions without having to take "center stage" for a presentation).

Return to the purpose. Say: "Becoming an expert and sharing what you have learned will help everyone in our class to know more."

Independent/Paired Activity

1. Have students choose a type of speech and topic they are interested in if they didn't already do so in the group activity.

2. Give students access to various forms of research (books, Internet, and experiential exposure). Students will do this activity over time, researching, studying, and taking notes; and writing and preparing speeches, props, and demonstrations to share with others in the class.

Let the Experts Explain

3. Ask students to make a list of new words or words they found very interesting during their research. Ask them to prepare a word list that has 5 of these words and can be distributed and shared with the class.

4. Have students share their expertise with others with a final presentation. Remind them that while presenting they are the teachers and the rest of the class are their students.

5. Give students a microphone if they want it.

6. Let students use props, pictures, music, or whatever is necessary to make their speeches interactive, engaging, and meaningful to themselves and the class.

7. Ask the class to use their active listening skills as they listen to the student or students who are speaking. Encourage them to take notes during the course of the presentation to help them recall information from the presentation when it is over. Have them think of and write down questions they might want to ask.

8. Give students the opportunity to ask questions of the presenters.

9. Create a "What We Have Learned Chart" on chart paper with each student's name. Have presenters ask the students to recall as much information as they can about the presentation. Have one student make a checkmark or put stickers next to the student presenter's name to represent all the details the students can recall about his or her topic.

Family Connections

1. Ask students to practice and present their speeches at home before giving them in class.

2. Invite families to the classroom so they can hear their students' speeches. You might create an evening classroom event for families titled "Let the Experts Explain!"

Word Magicians

Activity Overview

Word Magicians encourages students to use descriptive language while talking about specific words so that even if a word describes something that cannot be seen (e.g., friendship), the description will help others understand what the word is about. A concrete noun (e.g., dog, cat) names something that is tangible and can be seen or experienced through the senses. In contrast, an abstract noun (e.g., courage, freedom) names an idea, event, quality, or concept. This activity begins by helping a student to develop the ability to describe things that are concrete but not in the classroom (e.g., a pet at home) and leads to practice of descriptions of more abstract nouns such as friendship or loyalty.

> ### Materials • • • • • • •
> - Wizard's hat, magician's hat, or magic wand (can be just a straw or wooden dowel)
> - Drawing paper and markers
> - Timer

This activity gives students the opportunity to talk about something that is not present in the classroom or did not occur in the classroom. The topic could be a pet that is at home, a clown, or a waterfall they saw or read about, an event such as a party or parade, or it could ultimately be a concept such as courage. You can have younger students hold a magic wand when they are the Word Magicians, performing word magic and making word pictures "appear" before the listeners' very eyes. Older students can do this without the props. The description can be followed by having the other students draw what they have visualized.

Link to Literacy

Background knowledge impacts a students' ability to understand the language in books. For some students, who have limited first-hand knowledge of what they are reading about, it is difficult to create a mental image of the content in the text. Comprehension is enhanced when students can connect what they are reading to background knowledge they already have. Creating opportunities for students to practice speaking about things that are not physically present or a part of their background experience helps students to be more receptive when they encounter those concepts in text.

Whole-Class Activity I

Set the purpose. Say: "If we can describe things that aren't there and create images in the listeners' minds, it shows that our words have magical powers—they can make the invisible appear—and, we become word magicians!"

1. Model this activity yourself. Choose a topic that is relevant to your class, school, or community. If you have younger students, you can describe your favorite place to go camping, your dog, or an ice-cream sundae. If you have older children who are studying Native Americans,

you can describe what the inside of a tipi might have looked like. Even though students cannot see it in front of their eyes, they can still see it in their minds by listening to your words. For example:

- ↻ A tipi was used as a home for the Plains Indians.

- ↻ Near the center, a shallow hole was dug and lined with rocks, and this fire pit was used for cooking and warmth. There was an opening above it for the smoke to escape.

- ↻ Beds were made from buffalo skins and lined the walls of the tipi. The skins were also used as rugs.

- ↻ The walls were decorated with pictures and symbols that represented daily life and important beliefs and events, such as a buffalo hunt or a winding river.

Wave a magic wand and ask students what they are seeing in their minds. You might draw the tipi as they describe their images.

2. Choose one student to be the speaker.

3. Give the speaker a magician's or wizard's hat to wear or a wand to hold as they begin speaking. Tell him or her that he or she is now the "Word Magician."

4. **Say:** "Please try to make pictures in your mind as you listen to the words that are said by the word magician in the description."

5. Ask the Word Magician to describe something. (It can be a personal object that is not present in the classroom, such as a pet at home or his or her room. It can be what he did before coming to school, the night before, or at recess. It can also be something related to content: "Describe one challenge faced by the American colonists." "Describe the different states of water (solid, liquid, or gas).")

6. Have the speaker ask the other students if they have any questions, answer the questions asked, filling in gaps, and allowing for corrections in the pictures the listeners may have made.

7. Give out drawing paper to all the students who have been listening. Have them draw a picture that is based on the Word Magician's description.

Return to the Purpose. Say: "You have been using the magic of words to help each other make pictures in your minds of things that are not right in front of your eyes. Being able to see things that are not here in front of you will help you learn more about things that exist or existed in different parts of the world or in different periods of history."

Whole-Class Activity II

If you have older students, you can discuss the difference between concrete and abstract nouns.

1. Let students know that **concrete nouns** are what we generally think of as nouns, because a concrete noun is a person, place, or thing.

2. Tell them about **abstract nouns**. Describe that an abstract noun cannot be seen, heard, tasted, felt, or smelled, yet it can still be known and understood, such as a concept like bravery or friendship.

3. Talk to your class about the word **bravery**. It is an abstract noun. Describe someone you have studied or read about who has exhibited **bravery**.

4. Ask the students to make an image in their minds about what it means to be **brave**.

5. Ask them if they can help you describe what it means to be a **brave** person.

6. Make a web of words that relate to bravery (e.g., heroism, guts, courage, nerve, valor, daring).

7. Have students create sentences that relate to the concept.

Independent/Paired Activity

Use a timer to time the different parts of this activity. Tell the students to stop when time is up for each portion.

1. Have students choose or assign them to a Talking Buddy (or partner). Ask them to sit next to their partner.

2. Ask students to choose who will be the first speaker or Word Magician and who will be the first listener in the pair.

3. Give the speaker or Word Magician a magic wand. Give both students drawing paper and markers.

4. Assign a topic to the first Word Magician. Ask the Word Magician to describe it while the listener actively listens. (1-2 minutes)

5. Let the listener ask the Word Magician questions in order to fill in details or make corrections to his or her mental image. (1 minute)

6. Have the listener make a quick sketch of what was described by the Word Magician. (1 minute)

7. Have the Word Magician check the listener's image as he or she describes the sketch, using recalled information. For example, "This is your dog and he is big and has brown wavy hair, big brown eyes, and a long tail. He likes to sleep on your bed and loves dog treats." (1 minute)

8. Ask the partners to switch roles and repeat the activity. Give the new Word Magician a new topic. (5 minutes)

9. Have the partners return to their seats with their sketch and take out a piece of paper. Looking at their quick sketch, have them write a 3-minute description of their partner's topic.

Family Connections

1. Have students go home and describe something that is at school and their family members cannot see because it is at school.

2. Ask older students to have a discussion with family members about an abstract noun, such as **bravery** or **war**, and explain the difference to their families about concrete and abstract nouns.

Word Magicians

Every Picture Tells a Story

Activity Overview

Creating mental pictures is a foundational comprehension strategy that is critical for deeper understanding of text. Good readers make pictures in their minds as they read. Good listeners make pictures as they listen. They can then refer to these pictures as they are thinking about what they have heard or read. When students make pictures in their minds they can look back at them as reference for comprehension as well as a hook to help them recall words.

In the Every Picture Tells a Story activity, student speakers (describers) describe a picture they are holding, but listeners cannot see. Listeners work to create a mental image of the picture being described by speakers and retell the picture's story description using specific, guided retelling word prompts. The students refer to their retelling words for sequence and detail as they create a paragraph or series of sentences.

Materials

- Variety of pictures
- Retelling Word List (see Appendix A)
- Several sets of 10 index cards with one retelling word (who, what, where, when, why, size, color, sound, texture, and feeling) per card
- Short passages or stories to read aloud
- Plastic baggies
- Drawing paper
- Writing paper

Link to Literacy

Every Picture Tells a Story reinforces the use of pictures to support the understanding of information. The activity creates the basis for descriptive writing. Having a visual mental model is essential for comprehension.

Whole-Class Activity

Set the purpose. Say: "Good readers make pictures in their minds when they read. Making pictures in your mind helps you understand what you listen to and read. This activity will help you use mental pictures to understand and retell stories both aloud and in writing."

1. Choose a picture. Do not show the class the picture. Ask students to listen (they may close their eyes) and try to create a picture in their minds as you describe what you see in the picture for about a minute.

2. Show the picture to the class and get feedback about how their mental pictures compared to your actual picture.

3. Introduce the Retelling Word List. Put the words (who, what, where, when, why, size, color, sound, texture, and feeling) on the board in the front of the room. (You can also make copies for all students to place in their regular classroom writing folders or notebooks.) You can create your own retelling word list depending on your students' ability level (or use just a few of the words to start with). When students get comfortable, have them consider all of the words as they listen and retell. Talk about the words and explain that they will help you to do a more complete description with the second picture you are going to describe to them.

4. Explain to the class that this time when you describe the picture you will try to let the retelling words guide your description. Tell the students if you forget to tell them something, they can use the retelling words and remind you. For example: "You forgot to tell us how big the dog is in the picture." (size)

5. Choose a third picture and repeat this activity, doing a thorough job of describing the picture in terms of who, what, where, when, why, size, color, sound, texture, and feeling.

6. When you have finished your description, show the group the picture and ask the students to compare and contrast their mental images with the actual picture. Ask if the retelling words helped them in forming an image.

7. Read a highly visual passage to students. If you have *Visualizing and Verbalizing* by Nanci Bell, choose a passage at the correct level for your class.

8. Ask student questions based on mental images they make while you are reading. Questions will relate to the passage and tap into higher order thinking skills such as prediction, inference, and main idea. They can also relate to basic recall of things like color, size, and sequence. Use wording such as "In your picture, how big was the tree? Was it tall and skinny or wide with branches that spread out?"

Return to the purpose. Say: "Creating pictures in your minds will help you understand more when you listen and read."

Independent/Paired Activity

1. Have students work with partners.

2. Give each student pair a set of 10 retelling word index cards. Fewer cards can be given to younger or lower-level students.

3. Ask the students to decide who will be the first describer and who will be the first listener.

4. Give a picture to the first describer in each student pair.

5. Have the students spread the retelling words out on the floor or desk between them.

Every Picture Tells a Story

6. Have the student describer begin his description, and ask both students to check to see if the retelling words are guiding the describer.

7. Have the describer do this activity for about 1–2 minutes, then let the listener see the picture and compare his or her image to the actual picture.

8. Have the student pair work together to write down a paragraph or a series of sentences (depending on the level of the students) that describe or "tell the story" of the picture that was described.

9. Have the students change roles and repeat the activity.

Family Connections

1. Let students choose one or two of their favorite pictures from the classroom activity to take home for use with family members.

2. Have students make a set of retelling cards and put them in a plastic baggie to take home and use to practice the activity at home.

Choose Your Own Adventure

Activity Overview

Choose Your Own Adventure engages students in thinking deeply about an adventure they can create themselves or with a group of students. Students create an adventure that can be based on current direct class instruction or an extension of their own experience. They present the adventure story to their classmates and help to identify vocabulary that enhances the story while listening students draw pictures that represent their story. The opportunity to create their own adventure enhances interest, engagement, and motivation for the topic being studied and gives students the opportunity to experience ownership of the material.

The creation of the adventure enhances students' ability to speak and to write convincingly about what they have learned. Give students the option to study and take notes before presenting their adventures orally to others. Encourage them to include their fellow students in the presentation of their adventure stories by building in sections of the story ("crossroads" in the narrative) where they allow their classmates to choose between two options. This will give students who are presenting confidence in their ability to change or manipulate the direction of a story, and will also allow for cooperative learning between all students and encourage and stimulate active listening.

Materials • • • • • •

- Materials (books, videos, Web sites, and atlases) for researching the places and periods where the adventure will take place
- Adventure stories (fiction or nonfiction)
- Props to help bring the adventure to life
- Microphone
- Choose Your Own Adventure Worksheet (see Appendix A)
- Index cards with pictures of various places or index cards with time periods written on them

Link to Literacy

Choose Your Own Adventure supports literacy as students listen, watch, and read to gather information about the time, place, and period they are studying. Students engage more actively with text when they feel a personal purpose for reading. In composing and writing a narrative, students transfer what they have learned from the oral level to the written level. The knowledge base of the listeners is enhanced when fellow classmates share their adventures. The vocabulary of all students is enhanced with this activity since the student storytellers are exposed to new words during their research and presentations, and the student listeners are exposed to these same words as they listen to the final adventure story.

Choose Your Own Adventure

Whole-Class Activity I

Set the purpose. Say: "The more you know about things, the easier it is to learn more! Learning about other people and places helps you gain knowledge that will help you understand many other things. When you share your knowledge with others you are helping them get smarter and learn more also."

1. Read several short but effective adventure stories to your students. You might want to read one or two that involve making choices about the direction the story will take. This will get students interested in the adventure genre.

2. Read several short stories or passages that take place in different places and/or time periods. Choose one of the time periods and places and begin to make up your own adventure story.

3. When you come to a "crossroads" in the story, give students two choices and let them choose the direction your story will go.

4. Continue stopping and asking until you have completed your short adventure.

5. Make a list of some of the important vocabulary words you used in your adventure that are necessary to fully understand it.

6. Define them for the class.

7. Write the categories of the Choose Your Own Adventure Worksheet on the board and fill it in with the class.

Return to the purpose. Say: "The more you know about people and things they did, the easier it is to learn more things. You have been sharing information about people and their adventures, and you have all been learning more."

Whole-Class Activity II

The following are two sample adventure stories. The first, "Mary Elizabeth Makes a Friend," requires you to provide background building activities for the topic of life in colonial America, such as reading stories, showing videos, and introducing concepts. The second example, "The Adventures of Rosie the Pup," is a simpler story and is representative of an adventure story based on a student's experience. No background building activities are needed as it is just an extension of the student's experience.

Sample One: "Mary Elizabeth Makes a Friend"

1. After building background knowledge about life in Colonial America (through the use of videos and reading stories), ask students some questions to ensure understanding. Questions can be as follows:

   - Why did people come to the colonies?
   - What kinds of belongings did people bring with them?
   - How did people manage to survive the hardships they experienced when they arrived?
   - Would you want to leave your home to live in a country you know nothing about?
   - How do you think you would have felt if you had lived during Colonial times?

2. Following this background building, ask students to create an adventure story about a little girl who moves to colonial America with her family. Model the example below first, if needed.

Sample Story One

Mary Elizabeth Makes a Friend

Mary Elizabeth is a nine-year-old girl who lived in the colony of Plymouth in 1620. Her family settled in their new home after leaving England to find a better life. They traveled across the ocean in a large ship and they experienced many hardships during their voyage. There was not enough food and many people became ill. Although their voyage was difficult, when they reached their new country the family was very happy.

Mary Elizabeth's family had been city dwellers when they lived in England. However, now they were colonists, living in the colony of Plymouth, in a small wooden house in the woods. They had to learn how to grow their own vegetables and hunt for meat. Mary Elizabeth's mother sewed all of her clothing from homespun cloth. She wore a bonnet for protection from the sun and boots that were handmade by the local cobbler.

One day Mary Elizabeth wandered away from the colony and stumbled on a root that was sticking up from the ground. She fell to the ground and realized that she could not get up and walk home. Suddenly, a Native American girl who was riding on her Pinto pony saw Mary Elizabeth. She stopped her pony and got off to see if she could help. She was about the same age as Mary Elizabeth. She could not speak English, but the two girls understood each other by gesturing.

3. Ask students: "What do you think Mary Elizabeth is feeling when she meets the Native American girl? Do you think she is afraid of the stranger? Should she wait for someone from her own town to come? Should she let the new girl help her?" Finish the story based on student responses.

4. Give students a Choose Your Own Adventure Worksheet. Ask them to list some vocabulary words mentioned in the adventure story, such as **voyage**, **hardships**, **dwellers**, **ill**, **colonist**, **colony**, **homespun**, **cobbler**, **survive**, and **gesturing**.

5. Ask students for some of the vocabulary words they chose, write them on the board, and define the words for them.

6. Have them draw a picture of the adventure story on their worksheet. Ask them to label places on the picture that represent some of the vocabulary words.

Sample Two: "The Adventures of Rosie the Pup"

1. Ask students to think about an experience they recently had in their own lives that was an adventure or could have become an adventure.

2. Model the example of a personal adventure (next page). Tell students that as you tell them your adventure story you will need their help to continue the story. At certain points in the story you will ask them to choose from two different outcomes. In this way, students can participate in creating your adventure story and also get excited about creating their own.

Choose Your Own Adventure

Sample Story Two

The Adventures of Rosie the Pup

Yesterday my dog Rosie went out into the backyard to play. We live in the mountains and there are many interesting things like bushes and plants in our backyard. Rosie barked to come inside when she was ready. She hadn't been inside very long when she threw up. We were a little worried about her. But then she took a nap.

When she woke up. . . (**Choose:** *she was much better* or *she was getting worse*). When she woke up she was getting worse. Her balance was off and her coordination was poor. Whenever Rosie tried to walk she fell over or walked into things. We took her to the veterinarian right away and he said that she was having a toxic reaction. He thought that she may have eaten a poisonous mushroom.

The vet wanted to. . . (**Choose:** *keep her at his office* or *send her home to rest*). The vet wanted to keep her at his office so he could observe her behavior. He also gave her an injection of medicine and took her temperature.

When we got home, we looked in the yard and guess what we found? A mushroom that was half-eaten! The veterinarian had been correct. Rosie had eaten a poisonous mushroom and it had made her sick. We took her home later that day and she rested.

This morning Rosie got up and was walking around with a shoe in her mouth. I think she has recovered from her illness and is back to her normal puppyish self again!

3. Give students a Choose Your Own Adventure Worksheet. Ask them to list some vocabulary words mentioned in the adventure story, such as **worried, veterinarian, balance, coordination, toxic, poisonous, injection, puppyish, temperature**, and **normal**.

4. Ask students for some of the vocabulary words they chose, write them on the board, and define the words for them.

5. Have them draw a picture of the adventure story on their worksheet. Ask them to label places on the picture that represent some of the vocabulary words.

Independent/Paired Activity

1. Have students work in a small group or pairs or individually.

2. Have students choose a place and time for their adventure. For students who need more guidance, give them index cards with pictures of places glued on them (e.g., home, school, backyard, hospital, Greece, colonial America) or index cards with time periods written on them (e.g., day, night, weekends, ancient Greece, the 18th century) depending on what you have directly taught.

3. If students are paired or in a small group, have them work together to create their adventure. Ask them to create a fully-formed beginning-to-end adventure or create "choose" points in their adventure where the narrative can go different directions.

4. Give each group a toy microphone to use as a prop (inspiring confidence and credibility) when they tell their story. Ask students to share their adventures in different ways:

   ☺ The group can choose one member to read or tell the adventure.

- Each group member can read or tell a part of the adventure.
- The group can share pictures and props that go along with their adventure.
- The group can plan a skit to act out their adventures.

5. After the adventure story is shared, have the presenting students tell the class their story's special vocabulary words (words they themselves learned about while doing the research) and what they mean. Write the vocabulary words on the front board.

6. Repeat these steps for each group or pair in the class.

7. After each adventure story is shared, give out a Choose Your Own Adventure Worksheet to the students. Have them choose and write down 3–5 of the vocabulary words that they learned, or liked, from the vocabulary list on the board. Have them complete the worksheet by drawing a picture that reflects some important part of the adventure that was shared and including/referencing the vocabulary words in the picture they draw.

8. Students who have the written language skills can also write about the adventure. This can be done in a narrative form or can become a book project.

Family Connections

1. Encourage students to share their adventure with their families.

2. Encourage students to also share their new vocabulary words with their families by using the words in sentences and asking their family members to choose their three favorite words and create new sentences with them.

3. Encourage students to tell their families about one of the other adventures they heard in class and also share their favorite vocabulary words from that adventure with family members.

Choose Your Own Adventure

Section V:
Family Connections

O ral language development works best when parents are partners. This section gives you ideas about how you and your school community can help make parents work as partners to enhance their children's oral language skills. Parents want what is best for their children, but it is often our job to educate and give them guidance as to how they can support their children's academic achievement. Even when parents have weak oral language skills, they can help their children's oral language development by speaking more to them and increasing the number of positive statements they give them. If parents understand that doing this will support their children's academic achievement, they will work to do that. We often *tell* parents what we think they should do, but this section will give you actual activities to give to parents to *do* with their children. This simple shift can truly make a difference.

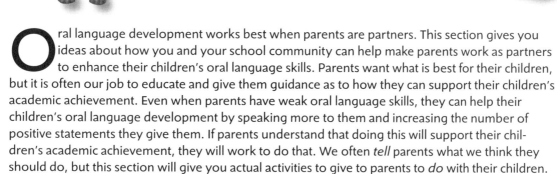

Family Words of Kindness

Activity Overview

Family Words of Kindness provides opportunities for family language time while it nurtures children's self-esteem and enhances expressions of appreciation within the family unit. Children come to school with very different affirmation experiences (Hart & Risley, 1995). This activity gives families a heightened awareness of the number of affirmations that are used in the home, while building opportunities for habits of positive and affirming communication to be formed. This activity is not about generating false and inauthentic praise, but rather offers opportunities for sincere expressions of kindness and gratitude.

Materials

- Self-stick notes
- Stationery
- Family Compliment Certificate (see Appendix B)

Link to Literacy

Oral language is the foundation for literacy development. Research suggests that children who come from lower socioeconomic households (Hart & Risley, 1995) are often exposed to fewer words and affirmations than other students. This activity attempts to increase the exposure to positive and affirming words students experience in the home. When children feel better about themselves, it increases the likelihood they will persevere and achieve positive results academically. This activity increases attention, listening, speaking, and writing through the use of positive communication. Increasing skill in these areas translates to higher levels of motivation, reading comprehension, and writing practice for children in the future.

Family Activity

1. Educate families at a school meeting, through notes home, and phone calls about the connection between positive statements to children and their self-confidence. Communicate to families that both positive statements and increased self-confidence can have a positive impact on academic achievement.

2. Send home self-stick notes, stationery, and Family Compliment Certificates. Model making affirming statements in your classroom so that students will be comfortable using the self-stick notes, stationery, and certificates at home.

3. Have students start the cycle of compliments by having them write a complimentary note for one or more family members on stationery in class and bring it home. (Students could also write notes and fill out a Compliment Certificate to bring home for different members of the family.)

4. At home, have students continue to ask family members to give compliments to each other using the self-stick notes, stationery, and Family Compliment Certificates.

5. At school, ask students to share who they gave compliments to and who they received compliments from in their household.

6. Ask students to get their parents to sign the Family Compliment Certificate and have them return it to school. If students consistently do not bring Compliment Certificates from their home, it is a sign that they need even more affirmations at school.

Family Words of Kindness

Family Backpack Notes

Activity Overview

Family Backpack Notes provides opportunities for positive interactions within the family while nurturing students' self-esteem and enhancing expressions of appreciation. Children come to school with very different experiences in terms of the number of positive statements they have heard (Hart & Risley, 1995). Family Backpack Notes offers families a way to increase the number of positive statements they make to their children on a daily basis.

Materials • • • • • •
- ◉ Self-stick notes
- ◉ Stationery

Link to Literacy

This activity gives families guidance to help them increase the positive statements they express to their children. Hearing more affirmations enhances children's self-confidence and increases the likelihood they will persevere and achieve positive academic results.

Family Activity

1. Discuss this simple activity with family members at a meeting or through written notes home. Make sure to emphasize the importance of positive and encouraging comments from parent to child.

2. Ask parents to surprise their children with written notes that are placed in children's backpacks. Give them some ideas for notes, such as:

   - ↻ Have a good day.
   - ↻ I love you.
   - ↻ Enjoy your lunch.
   - ↻ You are a great kid.
   - ↻ Thanks for clearing the dishes last night.
   - ↻ When you get home, let's talk about the day.
   - ↻ I want to hear all about your day.
   - ↻ I can't wait to hear about something fun you did today.
   - ↻ Thank you for being so kind.
   - ↻ Thank you for being so thoughtful.
   - ↻ Thank you for being so helpful.

- I love the way you give me big hugs.
- I love the way you ask about my day.
- I love the way you think of others.
- Let's play a game tonight.
- Let's read a book tonight.
- Let's take a walk after school.
- Let's bake cookies today.
- Let's cook dinner together tonight.

3. Ask children who receive notes from their parents to share them with the class.

4. If you have some children who are not receiving backpack notes, write some yourself and place them in the children's backpacks during the day.

Family Backpack Notes

Fair-Trade Book Fair

Activity Overview

The Fair-Trade Book Fair is a schoolwide activity that provides free books for the entire school population. Children's and adult books (in Spanish and English) are collected from all families that have books to donate; in addition, they can be collected from local places of worship and other organizations, such as Rotary and Kiwanis clubs. The books are then sorted by age, grade, and topic and are displayed in an organized and appealing fashion at the Fair. The Fair-Trade Book Fair should be open to the public just like any book fair. Encourage parents to come and shop for books for themselves and their children.

This activity gives all students, not just the ones who can afford them, a chance to have books at home. All students enjoy getting new books. Even students who have many books at home will be happy to trade them in for a few new ones.

Materials • • • • • •

- Book Fair Letter to Parents (see Appendix B)
- Solicitation letters to churches and other local organizations
- Parent volunteers for sorting and displaying books
- Prizes for classes that bring in the most books for the sale. This could be a pizza or popcorn party for the class with the greatest participation and success in the book collection project.

Link to Literacy

The Fair-Trade Book Fair encourages reading at home. Reading to children and having them read independently at home encourages vocabulary development, fluency, and supports literacy skill development and language comprehension.

Family Activity

1. Discuss the Book Fair with your class to get them excited about the idea of trading books with everyone else in the school. Tell them the principal, the workers in the cafeteria, and the gym teacher will all be participating in the Book Fair.

2. Send out the Book Fair Letter to Parents requesting any and all books they might have at home that can be donated to the Book Fair. Also ask for volunteers to "work" the Book Fair. Have the letter translated into Spanish if you have a number of Spanish-speaking families in your school.

3. Some schools may not have many families who have books to donate. If this is the case, send another letter requesting books to other organizations in your area, such as churches, synagogues, mosques, and Rotary and Kiwanis clubs. Keep a careful count during the collection process so that classes can compete for prizes.

Family Connections

4. Once books are collected, have parent volunteers sort and set up the Book Fair in the room where it will be held.

5. Dedicate several days and an evening to the Book Fair, just as you would for a typical book fair.

6. Give students lots of opportunities to go and choose books at the fair. To make sure that parents can attend the Book Fair, make sure you extend it into the late afternoon and evening hours (you might even consider a Saturday morning).

7. Give whatever books are left over to local charities.

8. As a classroom extension activity, encourage your students to bring books in to trade and share on a regular basis by having a book-trading corner in your classroom.

Fair-Trade Book Fair

Family Car Talk Topics

Family Homework Note

Date:
Homework/Topic:
What did you talk about?
What did you learn from your family conversation?
Signature of family member:

Activity Overview

Family Car Talk Topics encourages families to talk more during driving time together. Often when children get into their parent's car the radio is on or they watch DVDs. Older students may listen to their MP3 players. This activity encourages purposeful conversation in the car and opens the door to a establishing a habit of car-time conversation.

Materials

- Picture, topic, or objects for prompts
- Prompts related to school content areas
- Family Homework Note (see Appendix B)
- Family Conversation Starters (see Appendix B)

Link to Literacy

Family Car Talk Topics exposes children to more words, which facilitates literacy development. This activity helps parents understand that spending time talking to their children is beneficial and will help them in school.

Family Activity

1. Let parents know that talking to their children will benefit them in terms of school achievement. This is best done at a meeting with them, reinforced through notes and phone calls.

2. Tell parents to expect family homework that will involve simply talking to their children. Let them know that you would really appreciate it if they would sign the Family Homework Note and have their child return it to school the next day.

3. Give parents a list of topics (see Family Conversation Starters in Appendix B) and let them know that you will be choosing various topics for car talk. If they want to use a topic that is more meaningful to them, they can talk about that instead of the assigned topic.

4. Ask students to write something or share information orally (depending on the level of the student) about what was discussed in the car.

Family Connections

5. If a family is unresponsive to this activity, it is a sign to you that it is really important to find time to have conversations with that child in the classroom. You might try reviewing the 30-Second Conversation, Random Words of Kindness, and The Compliment Box activities for ideas.

Family Car Talk Topics

Family Select and Connect

Activity Overview

Family Select and Connect is an activity that uses a collection of pictures, or names and words, or phrases that involve family history and interests. Students can use a camera to take pictures of their family members. Disposable cameras can be available for loan to families who do not own a camera. Students work with their families to come up with words and phrases that are related in some way. The words and pictures are placed on a page or on index cards. The cards are lined up into two columns. Then, the students and their family members select two words (or a picture and a word) from each column and connect them in a meaningful way. For example, the words **Maria** and **scream** could be connected in the sentence: "Maria always screams when she sees a spider." Or, the words **Papa** and **scream** could be connected in the sentence: "Papa comes running when he hears Maria scream because he knows he will have to do something about a spider!"

Materials . . . .

- ◉ Index cards
- ◉ Photos
- ◉ Camera
- ◉ Yarn
- ◉ Select and Connect Worksheet (see Appendix A)

Link to Literacy

Making connections between two ideas and concepts is good practice for making connections during reading. When children flexibly match pictures and words, they can then use this knowledge to create interesting sentences and stimulate conversation.

Family Activity

1. Send a disposable camera home with students who do not have a camera at home. Ask students to take photos of their family members. If they already have photos of their family members, they can use the ones they have at home.

2. Have students bring in family photos and mount them on index cards at school to prepare for this family activity. You may need to have the pictures printed for your students, depending on their individual situations.

3. When the cards are prepared, students can be sent home with them and also some blank index cards. Also, give them some yarn to move between the index cards as they make connections.

4. Have students and their family members decide on words that relate to their overall family, and to individual family members, and put those words on some of the blank cards.

Family Connections

5. Have students set the index cards up into two columns.

6. Have them make three connections by moving the yarn three times between two index cards, one in each column, to represent the connections they are making.

7. Ask students to write down the three connections they've made on a separate piece of paper and create a sentence for each.

8. Another approach is to have the students use and fill in the Select and Connect Worksheet.

9. Have a family member sign either the separate piece of paper or the completed Select and Connect Worksheet and ask students to bring it back to class the next day.

Family select and Connect

Family Read Aloud Time

Activity Overview

Family Read Aloud Time is an activity that encourages parents to read to their children and listen to their children read to them. It also honors and supports family storytelling. In this activity parents are asked to dedicate time each day (or a few evenings a week) to read to their children. If the parents cannot read, they can listen to their children read to them, tell their children oral stories, or listen to taped stories together. Another approach for parents who are not able to read to their children is to arrange for older siblings to read to their younger siblings.

Materials ● ● ● ● ● ● ●

- Family Lending Library (fiction and nonfiction books that can be borrowed from the classroom for family reading time at home)
- Parent Read Aloud "Talking Points" (see Appendix B)
- Family Read Aloud Log (see Appendix B)

Link to Literacy

Listening to language is linked to literacy achievement. The more words that have washed over children, the more language they can understand and use themselves. Because there is often a vast difference in the number of words children of different socioeconomic status have been exposed to, reading to students in class can begin to close the language exposure and comprehension gap.

Children who can read still love to be read to by their teachers and families. However, once children can read, combining reading to them with reading independently and reading to their family members, is a helpful approach. The research of Keith Stanovich and Anne Cunningham (1998) informs us that the amount of independent reading done by fluent readers and non-fluent readers varies tremendously. Weak readers need the most practice, but, in actuality, get the least practice. Students in the 90th percentile for reading achievement actually read as many words in two days independently as the students in the 10th percentile read in a year. Explaining the importance of reading practice to parents can be very helpful in getting them to cooperate and provide "read aloud time" for their children.

Family Activity

1. Initiate a process of educating parents and family members about the connection between reading to children and reading achievement. Explain that the more language children are exposed to, the more language they will be able to understand when reading school books, assignments, tests, newspapers, and magazines.

2. Ask families to make a commitment of dedicated time a certain number of nights each week for reading to and with their children.

Family Connections

3. Provide a rotating Family Lending Library for books that can be borrowed from the classroom for Family Read Aloud Time.

4. Explain to parents the importance of talking to their children about the books they are reading. Send home the Parent Read Aloud "Talking Points" for parents to use as a reference.

5. Send home a Family Read Aloud Log weekly, or you can decide how often you want this done to add accountability to this family activity.

6. Regularly ask students to share information about what they read to their parents or siblings or what was read to them most recently.

7. If you find that you have a family that is not providing read aloud time for their child, arrange to have an older student or school volunteer read to that child during certain prearranged and regular periods of time each week. This will ensure that all students in your class are given extra oral language exposure, even if their families are not providing that time and exposure.

Family Read Aloud Time

Family Chatter Chips

Activity Overview

Family Chatter Chips provides opportunities for family language time while nurturing children's self-esteem and enhancing honest and authentic communication. Family communication enhances student achievement by exposing children to more words and putting the words they hear in meaningful contexts that relates to family experiences.

This activity structures communication so that there is always a framework to make communication easier and more comfortable, even for families in which communication is limited. Students create questions in class to make a

Materials • • • • • •

- ❧ Index cards, scissors, and glue
- ❧ Family Chatter Cards
- ❧ Family Chatter Reward Coupon (see Appendix B)
- ❧ Family Chatter Chips (these may be plastic chips, cut up paper, pennies, etc.)
- ❧ Family Homework Note (see Appendix B)

deck of attractive Family Chatter Chips to take home for family use. These authentic, child-generated questions touch on their own areas of interest and concern. Students may choose to use all the questions they create or only the ones they think will be meaningful to their family. Students will also bring home Reward Coupons so that the family member who accumulates the most Chatter Chips can get a reward from the other family members. These Reward Coupons can be generated by students in class, and blanks can also be taken home to be filled out by the family.

Link to Literacy

Research has shown that the playing field for children entering school from different socioeconomic groups is quite uneven in areas of vocabulary and oral language exposure. This activity exposes children to more words, more contextualized background knowledge, and more conversation. Oral language comprehension is tied to reading comprehension and oral and written language expression. This activity will make children feel more like communicators and enhance their willingness and ability to communicate in school-related activities.

Family Activity

1. Explain to students that they will be creating a game to take home and play with family members. The game should be lots of fun to play and will center around talking to each other and increasing how much family members know about each other.

2. Have students brainstorm and write questions and activities for their potential Family Chatter Cards. They may work independently, with a partner, or in small groups. Have them include

questions requiring oral answers, drawings, things acted out, singing, etc. Give them a couple of examples, such as:

- ℮ What is your favorite color?
- ℮ What is your favorite food?
- ℮ Draw a quick sketch of you doing your favorite activity.
- ℮ Act out how you would react if you won the lottery.
- ℮ What would you do with the money you got if you won the lottery?
- ℮ If you could change the world, what are three things you would do?

3. Have students share all the questions and activities that they create with the class.

4. Compile a list of everything that is created and shared by the students, all the "potential" Family Chatter Cards. Print out a copy of the list for each child.

5. Give students index cards and have them cut and paste the questions they want to include from the list onto their individual family deck of Chatter Cards.

6. Let students decorate the back of their cards or give them a Family Chatter Cards logo that your class makes up.

7. Before explaining the rules of the Family Chatter Chip game to students, remind them that it is their responsibility to make sure family members answer the Chatter Chips in complete sentences! Be sure that you have already given direct instruction and practice in how to build complete sentences. Giving this responsibility to the children will increase their own awareness of what it means to speak in complete sentences. Practice this with your class before they take the games home.

8. The rules of the game can vary, but children can follow these rules to begin with (model the game once in class if needed):

a. Have students place a stack of Family Chatter Cards in the middle of the table.

b. Choose who will go first.

c. Place chips in the middle of the table. The number will vary depending on the number of people playing (20–30 chips is probably appropriate for 3–4 players).

d. Students have family members take turns turning over one Family Chatter Card at a time and responding to the question on the card.

e. If the family member gives a response within one minute, then he or she gets a chip.

f. If the response goes beyond the question to include extra information, then that person gets an extra chip. Modeling this with your students in class is a good idea. Have them answer a Chatter Card question in a basic way, then have them practice answering the same question with extra information. For example: *My favorite color is blue.* = 1 chip *My favorite color is blue. I like the color of the sky when it is bright blue without any clouds.* = 2 chips

Family Chatter Chips

g. The play continues for either a designated amount of time or until the cards are used up.

h. The person with the most chips earns a Family Chatter Reward Coupon and can designate who will fill out and determine his or her reward.

9. Have students prepare some Reward Coupons ahead of time and encourage them to bring some blank coupons home. Ask them to have their family jointly decide what some good rewards would be for individual family members, such as: a big hug, a goodnight kiss, a bedtime story, washing the dishes, an ice-cream cone, or breakfast in bed.

10. Ask students to fill out and return a signed Family Homework Note to school the next day. Ask them to share some of the best communication that occurred during the game.

Family Table Topic Talk

Activity Overview

Family Table Topic Talk encourages families to talk more. Often families eat dinner on the run or in front of the TV. This activity encourages families to designate a few evenings a week for eating together as a family seated at a table. This family time can then be used for authentic conversation and will open the door to establishing a future habit of table-time talk.

Materials • • • • • • •

- ◎ Picture, topic, or objects for prompts
- ◎ Prompts related to school content areas
- ◎ Family Homework Note (see Appendix B)
- ◎ Family Conversation Starters (see Appendix B)

Link to Literacy

Family Table Topic Talk supports literacy development by exposing children to more words. This activity helps parents understand that spending time talking to their children is beneficial and will help them in school.

Family Activity

1. Educate parents about the relationship between talking to their children and school achievement. This is best done at a meeting and reinforced systematically over time through future meetings, notes, and phone calls.

2. Tell parents to expect family homework that will involve simply talking to their children.

3. Let parents know that you want them to sign the homework assignments and have their children return these signed notes to school the next day.

4. Give parents a copy of the Family Conversation Starter page and let them know that you

Family Table Topic Talk

will be choosing various topics for table talk. If they have one that is more meaningful to them, they are welcome to talk about that instead of the assigned topic.

5. Ask children to write something either at home or at school the next day (depending on the level of the child) about what was discussed at the dinner table.

Family Stories

Activity Overview

Family Stories provides families with a framework to use while they share personal stories. This activity encourages positive communication within families.

Link to Literacy

Family Stories encourages child-parent communication in the home in order to develop the child's oral language. The activity encourages teachers to systematically educate parents about the fact that speaking is the foundation for reading comprehension and academic success. In addition, this activity encourages positive interactions in the home, further enhancing the child's confidence as a learner.

Materials • • • • • • •

- ◉ Photos or drawings of family members
- ◉ Tape recorder
- ◉ Drawing paper
- ◉ Invitation to parents to come to class for story sharing

Family Activity

1. Have students ask family members to share a story. Send tape recorders home with children so they can have family members record their stories for easier sharing later with their classmates. This is also an effective way to get parents or family members who are not always available due to work schedules, etc., to participate on their own time.

2. Have students write down the story they are told, or make a picture that depicts something important about the story, so they can share and retell it at school.

3. Invite the family member to come to class and tell the story to the whole class. Encourage the class to ask questions and be responsive to any family member who is willing to share a story.

Family Stories

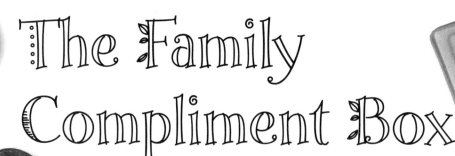

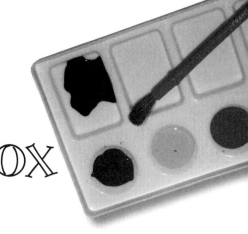

The Family Compliment Box

Activity Overview

The Family Compliment Box encourages affirmations within the family setting. Authentic affirmations boost confidence and allow students to move out of the family setting with a more positive attitude about their ability to learn and take risks in the school setting.

Materials......

- Compliment Box (use milk cartons, gift boxes, shoe boxes, or tissue boxes)
- Paint, markers, glitter, buttons, and glue
- Note paper
- Family Homework Note (see Appendix B)

Family Activity

1. Have students create a Compliment Box in school that can be used at home. It can be a milk carton, gift box, shoe box, or tissue box. Sometimes boxes shaped like treasure boxes can be found at hobby stores. Have students decorate their Compliment Box with paint, markers, glitter, buttons, etc.

2. Have students take home pieces of note paper for compliments.

3. At home, ask students and their parents to use the Compliment Box to make positive comments about each other, writing their positive comments on the note paper, and adding them to the box on an ongoing basis.

4. Encourage families to read the compliments in the box to each other on a regular basis.

5. Periodically, ask parents to send in their child's Family Homework Note with one of the compliments written on it.

6. Have students occasionally share their family compliments with the class.

7. If a student does not have a family that is doing this activity, make sure to give him or her more affirmations during the school day.

Appendix A

Worksheets

Buddy Talk Worksheet

Making connections to words you are learning will help you to remember them and be able to use them in your speaking and writing.

Write your target words or phrases on the lines below:

1. _____

2. _____

3. _____

4. _____

5. _____

You will be reading a passage or story. As you read, look for the target words. When you come to the target words or phrases underline them or put a self-stick note on the page where you have found the target word.

When you have finished your reading do 2 things:

1. Take turns with your partner using each target word in a sentence. Share a connection you have with the word or phrase.

2. Choose 2 target words, one for each of you, and create a sentence for each word. Write it down on the lines below.

   a. _____

   _____

   b. _____

   _____

Becoming a Good Listener, Speaker, and Writer

I. Becoming a Good Listener:

I will look at the speaker.

I will remain just as active when I listen as I am when I am speaking.

I will not interrupt until the speaker is done with his or her turn.

I may nod my head to show that I am following along.

I may ask questions that relate to what the speaker has said when there is a pause in speaking.

I may share my own connection with what the speaker has just said.

II. Becoming a Good Speaker:

I will look at the listener.

I will check to see if the listener understands me:

- ☺ Is he or she looking at me?
- ☺ Is he or she nodding?
- ☺ Does he or she look confused?

I can ask questions of the listener to check if he or she understands me, such as:

- ☺ Is that clear?
- ☺ Do you follow me?
- ☺ Do you have any questions?

I may use gestures to clarify what I want to communicate.

I may change my voice to help express and clarify what I want to communicate.

I will plan time for the listener to be able to respond to what I have said.

III. Becoming a Good Writer:

I will remember that the words I think about and say are connected to the words I will write down.

I will think about what I want to write in my head.

I will picture what I write as I think about it.

I will talk about what I am going to write to my teacher or classmate.

I will draw pictures, make a story map, or fill in a graphic organizer before I start to write.

I will share my writing aloud with my classmates, then add or change my writing if needed.

I will make a final copy of my writing with any changes to make it just right!

Select and Connect Worksheet

Name: _____

Select and Connect Words

1. _____   6. _____

2. _____   7. _____

3. _____   8. _____

4. _____   9. _____

5. _____   10. _____

My Favorite Connections

1. _____   6. _____

2. _____   7. _____

3. _____   8. _____

4. _____   9. _____

5. _____   10. _____

Painting Pictures Together Worksheet

My Subject: _____

_____

_____

149

All Ears for Idioms Worksheet

Idiom: _____

What it sounds like it means:	What it really means:

_____

_____

_____

Flyswatter Sentences Worksheet

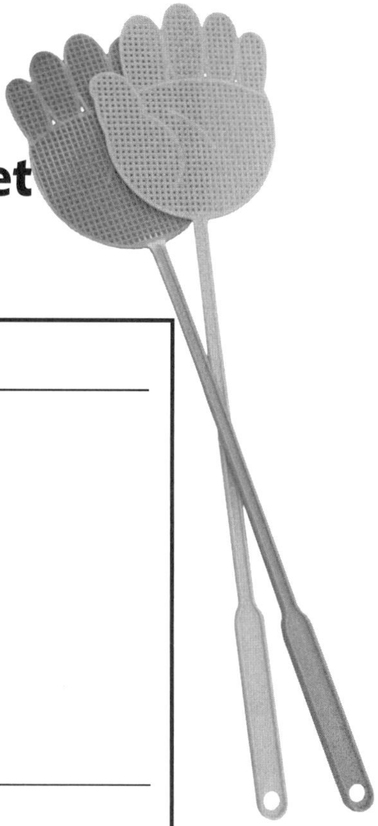

Word:_____

Sentence:_____

_____

_____

Word:_____

Sentence:_____

_____

_____

Word:_____

Sentence:_____

_____

_____

Word:_____

Sentence:_____

_____

_____

Word Web Sentences Worksheet

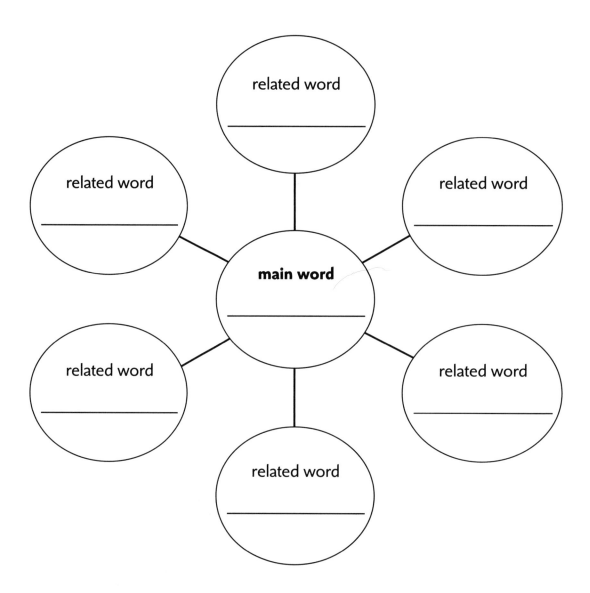

Touch the words that you use in your sentences.

1. _____

   _____

2. _____

   _____

ABC...Talk to Me Word List

A = apple, angry, alligator, ape, answering

B = banana, boy, bridge, bicycle, baking

C = cat, calendar, cast, corn, calculator, cutting

D = dog, dinosaur, dragon, dress, dancing

E = elephant, engine, edge

F = fox, fairy, fringe, finger, fishing

G = goat, girl, glass, grass, galloping

H = horse, heart, hand, hopping

I = iguana, ice cream, igloo, ice skating

J = jellyfish, jacks, jam, jumping

K = kangaroo, kite, kettle, kicking

L = leopard, lamp, lightning, licking

M = monkey, mask, map, mending

N = needlefish, nest, needle, napping

O = octopus, oven, oatmeal, opening

P = penguin, painting, planet, planting

Q = quail, quilt, queen, quacking

R = rhinoceros, ring, rainbow, rowing

S = snake, sew, snap, stitching

T = tiger, tank, track, tap dancing

U = urchin crab, umbrella, ukulele, using

V = veiled chameleon, van, vast, vanishing

W = walrus, weather, wax, watering

X = x-ray, xylophone

Y = yak, yesterday, yellow, yelling

Z = zebra, zoo, zone, zippering

Magnetic Sentences Tracking Mat

Worksheet 10

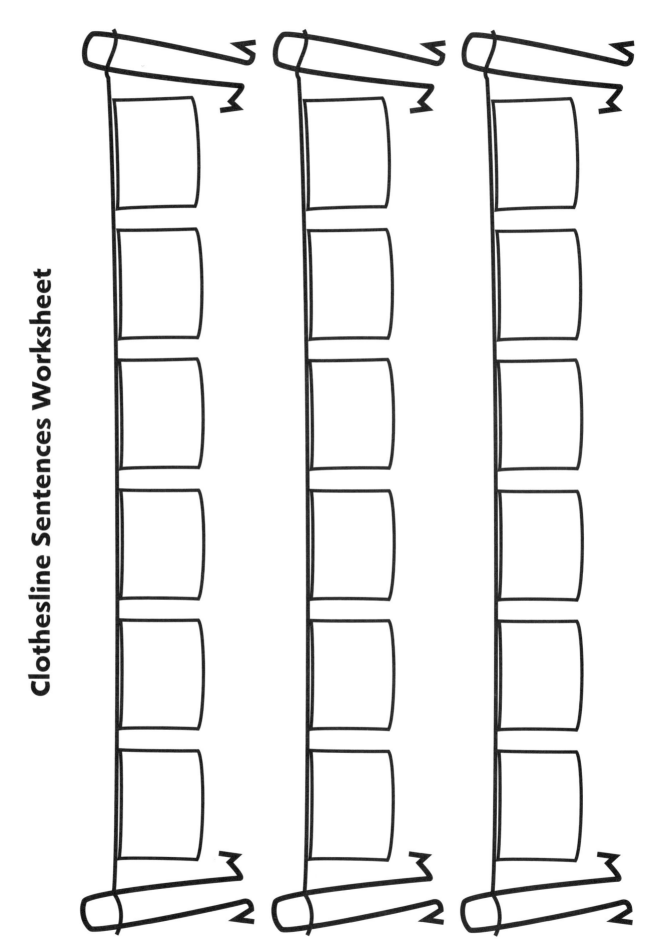

Clothesline Sentences Worksheet

Chain-Link Sentences Worksheet

e   Place this worksheet in a plastic sheet protector.

e   Use a dry-erase marker and place each word in your sentence in a separate link of the chain.

e   Rewrite the noun in a different color marker.

e   Rewrite the verb in a different color marker.

e   Write the whole sentence on the line below.

e   You may want to recopy your chain-link sentence on real paper links and choose different colored links for your nouns and verbs.

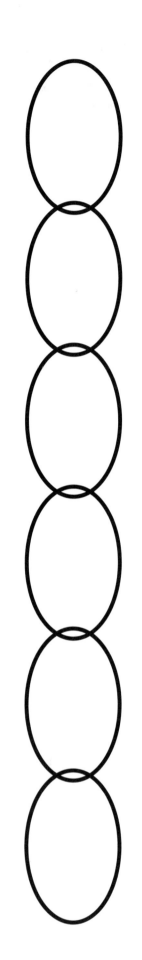

Language on a Roll Worksheet

First Roll = _____

_____

_____

Second Roll = _____

_____

_____

First Roll = _____

_____

_____

Second Roll = _____

_____

_____

First Roll = _____

_____

_____

Second Roll = _____

_____

_____

Sentence Ball Toss Picture Worksheet

Word Family Sentences Worksheet

Partner 1

1. Choose some word family words.

_____

2. Create a sentence using your word family words.

_____

_____

3. Draw a picture that represents your Word Family Sentence.

Partner 2

1. Choose some word family words.

_____

2. Create a sentence using your word family words.

_____

_____

3. Draw a picture that represents your Word Family Sentence.

Grammar-Go-Round Sentence Building Worksheet A

Who:

Noun

What:

Verb

Noun: Tell me more!

Adjective

Verb: Tell me more! How or with whom

Adverb

Grammar-Go-Round Sentence Building Worksheet B

Tell me where!

Tell me why!

Rewrite your sentence:
_____

_____

Ask a question about your noun!

Ask another question!

Write your questions:
_____

_____

Carousel of Knowledge Planning Guide

My Topic: _____

Who: _____

What: List three important facts about your person or topic.

   1. _____

   2. _____

   3. _____

Where: If you are studying a person, where did he or she live and where did important events occur?

_____

_____

_____

When: If there are important dates related to your person or topic, list and explain them here.

_____

_____

_____

Why: Write several sentences about why your person did the things he or she did. What was his or her motivation? Why do you find it interesting?

_____

_____

_____

_____

_____

Presentation Planning:
- What are you going to do as a group?
- Write and read a book about the topic.
- Write a skit and present it to the class.
- Write a song that has words that express the highlights of the topic.
- Write a report to present to the class.

Carousel of Knowledge Planning Wheel

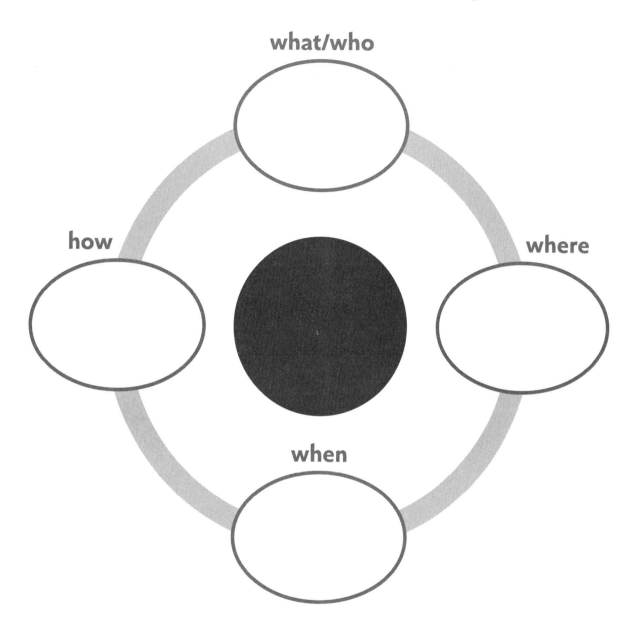

Getting to Know My Family Worksheet

Name of Family Member: _____

Relationship to you: _____

   1. Where were you born? _____

   2. When were you born? _____

   3. What do you enjoy doing? _____

   _____

   4. Who do you enjoy doing things with? _____

   5. What do you hope for in the future for yourself? _____

   _____

   _____

   6. What do you hope for in the future for the world? _____

   _____

   7. What is something you have done to help another person?___

   _____

   8. What is a funny story that happened to you? _____

   _____

   9. What is something that you believe in?_____

   _____

   10. What do you use for your job or your hobby?_____

   _____

   11. What is your favorite gift to give someone? _____

   _____

Reflections on My Learning

1. What is your favorite part of today's lesson?

   My favorite part of today's lesson is _____

   _____.

2. What part of the lesson connects to something you already knew?

   I already knew about _____ and I connected that with what I

   learned today about _____.

3. What was the most interesting new thing you learned today?

   The most interesting new thing that I learned today is _____

   _____.

4. What is something you would like to learn more about?

   I want to learn more about _____ .

5. Was there any part of the lesson today that confused you?

   The part of the lesson that confused me was _____

   _____.

Reflections on My Learning Venn Diagram

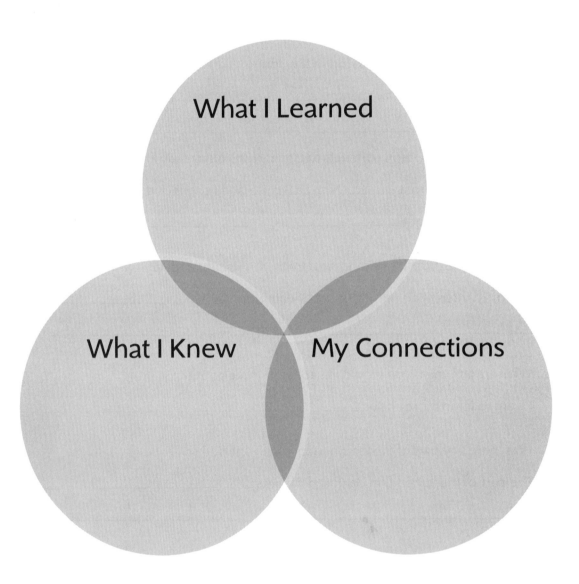

What I Learned

What I Knew

My Connections

Heroic Conversations Worksheet

Name of my hero: _____

Where my hero lived: _____

Heroic acts he or she performed: _____

_____

_____

_____

Heroic character traits of my hero: _____

_____

What I admire about my hero: _____

_____

_____

What I have learned from studying about my hero: _____

_____

_____

How can I be heroic? _____

_____

_____

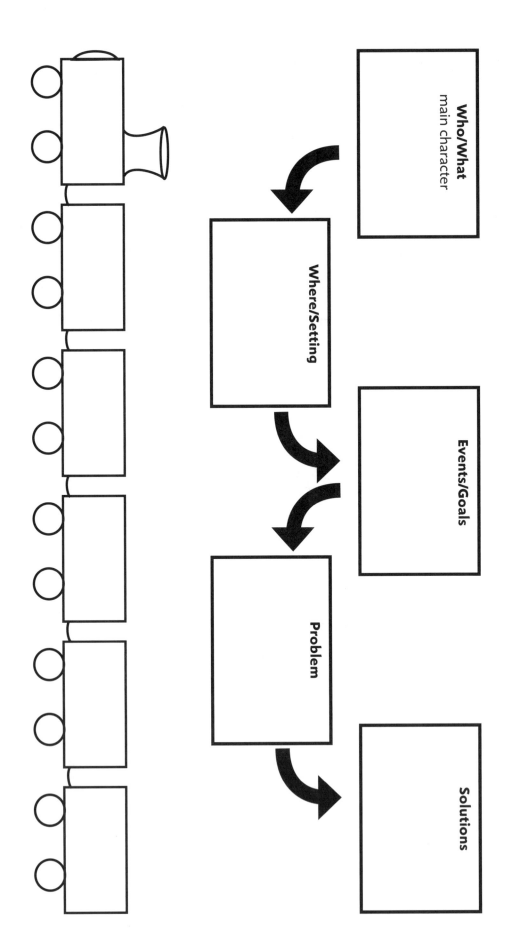

Story Train Worksheet

Story Cards use Story Grammar to Guide Oral and Written Retelling

Who/What
main character

Where/Setting

Events/Goals

Problem

Solutions

Retelling Word List

1. **Who**

2. **What**

3. **Where**

4. **When**

5. **Why**

6. **Size**

7. **Color**

8. **Sound**

9. **Texture**

10. **Feeling**

Choose Your Own Adventure Worksheet

Name the Adventure:

_____

Vocabulary Words (List the words below and then label them in the picture you draw.)

1. _____

2. _____

3. _____

4. _____

5. _____

Draw a picture of the Adventure Story you heard.

Appendix B
Teacher Materials

BLISS Strategy

◎ **B**uild background knowledge about a topic.

◎ **L**isten actively and speak responsively about the topic.

◎ **I**ntegrate and connect old knowledge with new learning.

◎ **S**how your knowledge through speaking, sorting, creating, and writing.

◎ **S**hare your knowledge about the topic by reading and sharing your work aloud orally.

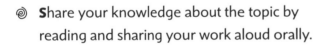

Compliment Certificate

Awarded to: _____

for expressing

Random Words of Kindness

Date: _____

Approved by: _____

The Ladder Template

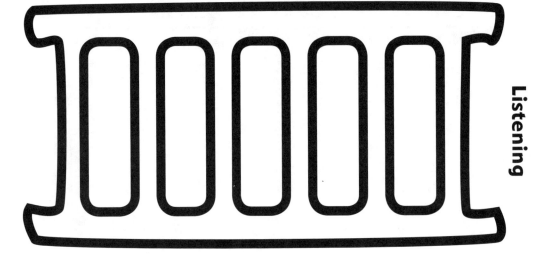

Listening

Speaking

Writing

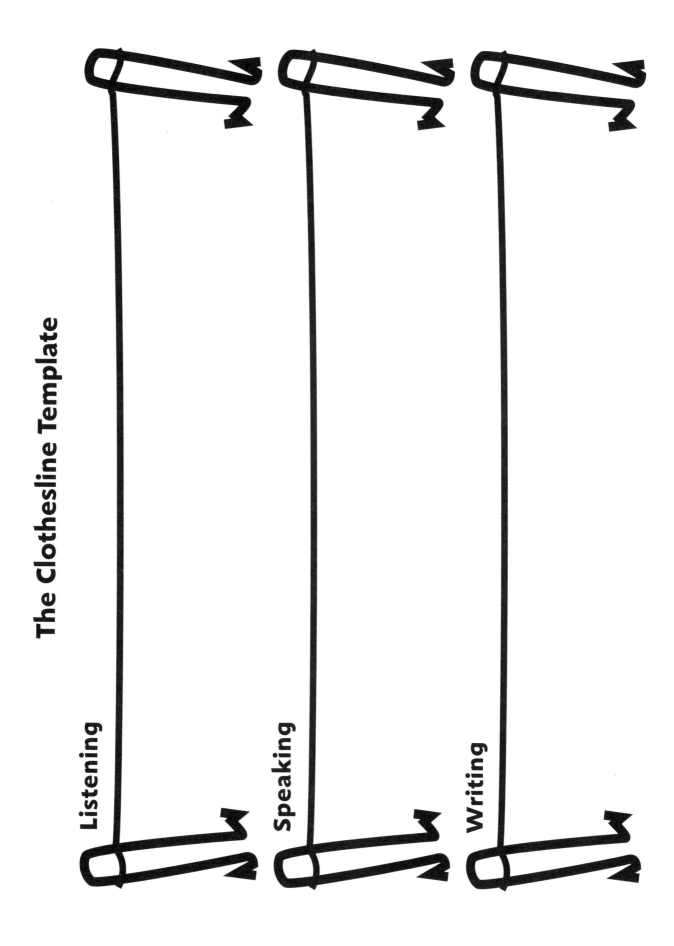

The Clothesline Template

Listening

Speaking

Writing

Vocabulary Connections Word List

A chair is almost like a couch, but not quite because...

A bowl is almost like a basket, but not quite because...

A clock is almost like a watch, but not quite because...

A tent is almost like a house, but not quite because...

A flag is almost like a kite, but not quite because...

A glass is almost like a cup, but not quite because ...

A shoe is almost like a boot, but not quite because...

A "P" is almost like a "B," but not quite because...

A bush is almost like a tree, but not quite because...

A car is almost like a truck, but not quite because...

A boat is almost like a ship, but not quite because...

A gate is almost like a door, but not quite because...

A card is almost like a book, but not quite because...

Sample Idiom List

Be up and running

Bent out of shape

Hit the road

Bite off more than you can chew

Blow your top

Break someone's heart

By the skin of one's teeth

Catch some Zs

Change one's mind

Down in the dumps

Drop him a line

Get a kick out of something

Hit the sack

Keep your chin up

Raining cats and dogs

Let sleeping dogs lie

Pull someone's leg

Read someone's mind

Family Homework Note

Date:_____

Homework/Topic:_____

_____

What did you talk about? _____

_____

What did you learn from your family conversation?

_____

_____

Signature of family member:_____

Family Homework Note

Date:_____

Homework/Topic:_____

_____

What did you talk about? _____

_____

What did you learn from your family conversation?

_____

_____

Signature of family member:_____

Proverbs List

A bird in the hand is worth two in the bush
A penny saved is a penny earned
A stitch in time saves nine
Absence makes the heart grow fonder
All that glitters is not gold
Beauty is only skin deep
Better late, than never
Better safe, than sorry
Birds of a feather flock together
Don't count your chickens before they're hatched
Don't cry over spilt milk
Don't judge a book by its cover
Don't look a gift horse in the mouth
Don't spit into the wind
Every cloud has a silver lining
He who hesitates is lost
If at first you don't succeed, try, try again
In unity there is strength
Look before you leap
Necessity is the mother of invention
Never put off till tomorrow what you can do today
One man's meat is another man's poison
One rotten apple spoils the barrel
Out of the frying pan and into the fire
People who live in glass houses shouldn't throw stones
Rome wasn't built in a day
Still waters run deep
The best way to a man's heart is through his stomach
The early bird catches the worm
The grass is always greener on the other side of the fence
The longest journey begins with a single step
Too many cooks spoil the broth
Two heads are better than one
When in Rome, do as the Romans do
Who holds the purse rules the house
You can lead a horse to water, but you cannot make him drink

A good additional resource for Spanish proverbs is:
http://cogweb.ucla.edu/Discourse/Proverbs/Spanish-English.html

Clothing Template

Word Family List

-an	-ack	-it	-ank	-ad
ban	back	bit	bank	bad
can	black	fit	blank	clad
clan	crack	hit	drank	dad
Dan	lack	it	plank	glad
fan	pack	kit	prank	had
man	rack	lit	rank	lad
pan	sack	pit	sank	mad
ran	snack	sit	tank	pad
tan	stack	slit	thank	sad
van	tack	spit	yank	tad

-ll	-ap	-en	-ip	-og
bill	cap	Ben	dip	bog
chill	clap	den	drip	cog
fill	flap	hen	flip	dog
hill	lap	men	hip	fog
ill	map	open	lip	frog
pill	nap	pen	rip	hog
spill	sap	then	ship	jog
still	slap	ten	sip	log
till	snap	when	skip	slog
will	tap	yen	trip	smog
	trap			

-op	-ot	-ug	-ump	-un
chop	dot	bug	bump	bun
drop	got	dug	clump	fun
flop	hot	hug	dump	gun
hop	lot	jug	grump	nun
mop	not	mug	hump	pun
plop	pot	plug	jump	run
pop	rot	rug	lump	shun
sop	spot	shrug	plump	spun
shop	tot	snug	stump	stun
stop	trot	tug	trump	sun
top				

Tips for Creating Engagement

1. Write and speak about:
   - Topics or people you have seen in videos, movies, or on TV (superheroes, historical characters, or real heroes).
   - Subjects you are studying (for example, American Colonists or Native Americans).
   - A story you have heard or read.
   - Personal subjects (pets, family, vacations, or hobbies).

2. Illustrate your stories.

3. Practice your story aloud.

4. Use prosody (change your voice to express fear, excitement, happiness, etc.).

5. Use gesture.

6. Use costumes and props.

7. Read the story to a small group or to the class if that makes you more comfortable.

8. Tell the story if you know it well enough.

Heroes Hall of Fame Certificate

_____
[NAME]

Is hereby inducted in to the Heroes Hall of Fame for his or her work:

_____

_____

Approved by: _____

Date: _____

List of Heroes

1. Martin Luther King Jr.
2. Mother Teresa
3. Jackie Robinson
4. Muhammad Ali
5. Albert Schweitzer
6. Jane Goodall
7. Wilma Rudolph
8. César Chávez
9. Elie Wiesel
10. Helen Keller
11. Nelson Mandela
12. Susan B. Anthony
13. Clara Barton
14. Eleanor Roosevelt
15. Rosa Parks
16. Mahatma Gandhi
17. Marie Curie
18. Arthur Ashe
19. Christa McAuliffe
20. Rachel Carson
21. The Dalai Lama
22. Archbishop Desmond Tutu
23. Jesse Owens
24. Aung San Suu Kyi
25. Bono
26. Jimmy Carter
27. Muhammad Yunus
28. Rigoberta Menchú Tum
29. Betty Williams
30. Adolfo Pérez Esquival

Speech Topics for Students

Informative Speech Topics

- Topics related to social studies, science, and math content
- Famous inventors and their inventions
- Artists and musicians
- Peacemakers and heroes
- Global issues (hunger, peace, etc.)
- How does the heart work?
- Why is the sky blue?

Demonstrative Speech Topics

- American Sign Language words
- How to make an ice cream sundae
- Tips to decorate your room
- How to wrap a birthday present
- How to decorate a cake
- How the pioneers packed their wagon on their westward journey

Persuasive Speech Topics

- How kindness can be taught and practiced
- Why recess should be longer
- Why we should recycle at our school
- Protecting the environment is important because

Family Compliment Certificate

Awarded to: _____

for expressing

Family Words of Kindness

Approved by: _____

Date: _____

Book Fair Letter to Parents

Dear Parents,

Our school is having our first Fair-Trade Book Fair. It is free to participate and the books are free. Students and their families can come to school and pick up books to take home with them. We will have books for babies, toddlers, school-age children, and adults.

If you have any books in your home that you are not using, please send them to school for our book fair. If you don't have any extra books at home please ask at your local place of worship. The class that collects the greatest number of books will get a prize.

Reading to your children is a great way to help them to become better readers. We know that all parents at our school want to help their children with their reading skills. Reading at home is fun and it can nurture your relationship with your children.

Please help us if you can by sending in books or magazines that we can give away at our Fair-Trade Book Fair. Regardless, please come and celebrate our book fair with us. Bring your children and get everyone in the family something good to read. For free!

Look for more details about the days and times of our book fair. Thanks for your support.

Sincerely,

Family Conversation Starters

Take the time for talking. Talking is better for children's academic and emotional development than listening to the radio, DVD, TV, or MP3 player. When you talk to your children, you *are* the main influence in their lives—not a public speaker or singer.

Listen without interrupting. Try to let your children finish *all* of what they are saying before beginning your response. Be sure that what you say is a response to what they have just told you.

Listen carefully. Listen to what your children might be saying "between the lines." For example, if one of your children is talking about someone being bullied at school, is that child really saying that he or she is afraid of the bully?

Ask their opinion. When you ask children for their opinion, it is a sign of respect for their thinking.

Here are a few ideas for conversation starters:

- What is your family tradition?

- Which famous athlete would you love to meet?

- What family rule do you think could be different?

- Ask specific questions about your child's day:
    - What was the funniest thing that happened today?
    - Who did you play with on the playground today?
    - Did you help anyone in your class today?
    - Did you say something nice to another student today?
    - What was the most interesting thing you learned today?

- Follow up the answer to these questions with other questions.

Encourage your child to make a list of the names of other children in the class. Place the list on the refrigerator at home, then ask specific questions about those students whose names are on the list.

Parent Read Aloud "Talking Points"

Fiction Talking Points:

1. Which character did you like the best? Why?
   (Tell your child which character was your favorite and why.)

2. Do any of the characters remind you of real people you know? Who? In what ways?
   (Make a connection yourself, telling who and in what way.)

3. Does this story remind you of any other stories you have heard or seen on TV or in the movies, or something that has happened in your life?
   (If it reminds you of something, share that with your child.)

4. Let's make believe we wrote this story. Could we come up with a different ending?

If this book is part of a series, decide together if you want to read more in the series. If you do, please alert the teacher and he or she may be able to help get the other books for you to check out.

Nonfiction Talking Points:

1. What did you learn that is most interesting to you?
   (Tell your child what you learned that was most interesting.)

2. What did you already know about this subject?
   (Tell your child something that you already knew [if anything] about the topic. Tell your child how knowing something about this topic before you started reading helped you to understand more about what you read.)

3. Do you want to read another book about this same topic?

4. Let's try to get another book about this topic.
   (Go to the library or ask the teacher.)

5. Let's try to see if we can find something on TV about this topic, as well.
   (Make a plan to find out more. Talk about what you want to read about next.)

Family Read Aloud Log

Week of: _____

Reading partners: _____

In the calendar below, list the books you read each day, how long you spent reading, and any comments.

Sunday	Monday	Tuesday	Wednesday	Thursday	Friday	Saturday

Family Chatter Reward Coupon

Awarded to:

_____

Your reward will be:

_____

_____

Signed:_____

Family Chatter Reward Coupon

Awarded to:

_____

Your reward will be:

_____

_____

Signed:_____

Family Chatter Reward Coupon

Awarded to:

_____

Your reward will be:

_____

_____

Signed:_____

Family Chatter Reward Coupon

Awarded to:

_____

Your reward will be:

_____

_____

Signed:_____

Observing Vocabulary Checklist

Student Name	Pronounces Words Correctly	Defines Word	Uses Word in Speaking	Uses Word in Writing	Connects to Related Words
1					
2					
3					
4					
5					
6					
7					
8					
9					
10					
11					
12					
13					
14					
15					
16					
17					
18					
19					
20					

Bibliography

Adams, G., & Brown, S. (2007). *The six-minute solution* (Primary Level). Longmont, CO: Sopris West.

American Speech-Language-Hearing Association Web pages.

Beck, I. L., McKeown, M. G., & Kucan, L. (2002). *Bringing words to life: Robust vocabulary instruction*. New York: The Guilford Press.

Beers, K. (2003). *When kids can't read — What teachers can do*. Portsmouth, NH: Heinemann.

Bell, N. (2003). *Visualizing and verbalizing stories*. San Luis Obispo, CA: Gander Publishing.

Blackenbery, T., & Pye, C. (2005). Semantic deficits in children with language impairment. *Jr. Language Speech and Hearing Services in Schools, 36*, 5016.

Bloom, L., & Lahey, M. (1978). *Language development and language disorders*. NY: John Wiley and Sons.

Corrales, O., & Call, M. E. (1989). At a loss for words: The use of communication strategies to convey lexical meaning. *Foreign Language Annals, 22*(3), 227.

Cunningham, A., & Stanovich, K. (1998). What reading does for the mind. *American Educator, 22*(1–2), 8–15.

Diffely, D., & Sassman, C. (2006). *Positive teacher talk for better classroom management*. NY: Scholastic Books.

Dodson, J. (2008). *50 nifty activities for 5 components and 3 tiers of reading instruction*. Longmont, CO: Sopris West.

Ebbers, S. M. (2007). *Power readers*. Longmont, CO: Sopris West.

Ebbers, S. (2009). *Daily oral vocabulary exercises (DOVE)*. Longmont, CO: Sopris West.

Gaiser, B. Meeting the Challenge of the Oral Language Gap. *Short Stories and tall tales by the princess and the pirate*. Video Learning Series, Lee County School District. Sandia@lee.k12.fl.us

Hart, T., & Risley, B. (1995). *Meaningful differences in the everyday experiences of young American children*. Baltimore, MD: Brookes Publishing.

Hirsch, E. D. (2006). *The knowledge deficit*. Boston: Houghton Mifflin.

Jackie Robinson Graphic Biography. (2008). Costa Mesa, CA: Saddleback Educational Publishing.

Lehr, F., Osborn, J., & Hierbert, E. (2004). *A focus on vocabulary*. Honolulu, HI: Pacific Resources for Education and Learning.

Moats, L. C. (2010). *Language essentials for teachers of reading and spelling (LETRS)*. Second Edition, Modules 1–7. Longmont, CO: Sopris West Educational Services.

Moats, L. C. (2005). *Language essentials for teachers of reading and spelling (LETRS)*. Modules 1–12. Longmont, CO: Sopris West Educational Services.

Mullen-Schneider, J., & Konrad-Weeks, M. (2004). *But not quite!* Seattle, WA: Toucan Creations, Inc.

National Institute of Child Health & Human Development (NICHD). (2000). Report of the National Reading Panel. *Teaching children to read: An evidence-based assessment of the scientific research literature on reading and its implications for reading instruction.* Washington, DC: National Institutes of Health.

Patrick, D. L. et al. (2005). Jackie Robinson strong inside and out. *Time for Kids Biographies.* New York, NY: Harper Collins Publishing.

Schneider, J. M., & Weeks, M. K. (2004). *But not quite.* Seattle, WA: Peanut Butter Publishing, an imprint of Classic Day Publishing, LLC.

Glossary

automaticity performance without conscious effort or attention; a characteristic of skill mastery

affix a meaningful part of a word attached before or after a root to modify its meaning

alphabetic principle the principle that letters are used to represent individual phonemes in the spoken word; a critical insight for beginning reading and spelling

alphabetic writing system a system of symbols that represent each consonant and vowel sound in a language

base word a free morpheme to which affixes can be added

chunk a group of letters, processed as a unit, that corresponds to a piece of a word, usually a consonant cluster, rime pattern, syllable, or morpheme

closed syllable a written syllable containing a single vowel letter that ends in one or more consonants; the vowel sound is short

consonant a phoneme (speech sound) that is not a vowel and that is formed by obstructing the flow of air with the teeth, lips, or tongue; English has 25 consonant phonemes

consonant blend adjacent consonants that appear before or after a vowel

consonant digraph a two-letter combination that represents one speech sound that is not represented by either letter alone (e.g., **sh**, **th**, **wh**)

consonant-le syllable a written syllable found at the ends of words such as dawdle, single, and rubble

cognitive desktop a figurative expression referring to the working memory capacity of the mind and the available attentional resources in consciousness

concept an idea that links facts, words, and ideas together as a coherent whole

context the language that surrounds a given word or phrase (linguistic context), or the field of meaningful associations that surrounds a given word or phrase (experiential context)

context processor the neural networks that bring background knowledge and discourse to bear as word meanings are processed

cumulative instruction teaching that proceeds in additive steps, building on what has previously been taught

decodable text text in which a high proportion of words (80%–90%) comprise sound-symbol relationships that have already been taught; used to provide practice with specific decoding skills; a bridge between learning phonics and the application of phonics in independent reading of text

decoding the ability to translate a word from print to speech, usually by employing knowledge of sound-symbol correspondences; also the act of deciphering a new word by sounding it out

dialects mutually intelligible versions of the same language with systematic differences in phonology, word use, and/or grammatical rules

digraph (see consonant digraph)

direct instruction the teacher defines and teaches a concept, guides children through its application, and arranges for extended guided practice until mastery is achieved

dyslexia an impairment of reading accuracy and fluency attributable to an underlying phonological processing problem

ELL English language learner

encoding producing written symbols for spoken language; also spelling by sounding out

explicit instruction instruction wherein the teacher defines the concept or association the student is to learn, provides guided practice with feedback, provides additional independent practice, and checks to see if the concept was learned, retained, and applied

expository text factual text written to "put out" information

grapheme a letter or letter combination that spells a phoneme; can be one, two, three, or four letters in English (e.g., **e**, **ei**, **igh**, **eigh**)

indirect vocabulary learning the process of learning words through incidental and contextual exposures, rather than through direct and deliberate teaching

integrated when lesson components are interwoven and flow smoothly together

long-term memory the memory system that stores information beyond 24 hours

Matthew Effect coined by Keith Stanovich; a reference to the Biblical passage that the "rich get richer and the poor get poorer," insofar as the pattern of language and reading skills development in individuals over time

meaning processor the neural networks that attach meanings to words that have been heard or decoded

meta-cognition the ability to reflect on and understand our own thought processes

meta-linguistic awareness an acquired level of awareness of language structure and function that allows us to reflect on and consciously manipulate the language we use

Glossary

morpheme the smallest meaningful unit of language

morphology the study of the meaningful units in the language and how they are combined in word formation

morphophonemic having to do with both sound and meaning

multisyllabic having more than one syllable

narrative text that tells about sequences of events, usually with the structure of a story, fiction or nonfiction; often contrasted with expository text that reports factual information and the relationships among ideas

orthographic processor the neural networks responsible for perceiving, storing, and retrieving the letter sequences in words

orthography a writing system for representing language

paraphrase express the thoughts in a sentence with different words

phoneme a speech sound that combines with others in a language system to make words

phoneme awareness (also phonemic awareness) the conscious awareness that words are made up of segments of our own speech that are represented with letters in an alphabetic orthography

phonics the study of the relationships between letters and the sounds they represent; also used as a descriptor for code-based instruction in reading (e.g., "the phonics approach" or "phonic reading")

phonological awareness meta-linguistic awareness of all levels of the speech sound system, including word boundaries, stress patterns, syllables, onset-rime units, and phonemes; a more encompassing term than phoneme awareness

phonological processor a neural network in the frontal and temporal areas of the brain, usually the left cerebral hemisphere, that is specialized for speech sound perception and memory

phonological working memory the "on-line" memory system that holds speech in mind long enough to extract meaning from it, or that holds onto words during reading and writing; a function of the phonological processor

phonology the rule system within a language by which phonemes can be sequenced and uttered to make words

phrase-cued reading the act of reading phrases that have already been marked or designated by underlining, spacing, or arrangement on the page

prefix a morpheme that precedes a root and that contributes to or modifies the meaning of a word; a common linguistic unit in Latin-based words

reading fluency the ability to read text with sufficient speed and accuracy to support deep comprehension

root a bound morpheme, usually of Latin origin, that cannot stand alone but that is used to form a family of words with related meanings

scaffolding providing extra structure or support that enables the learner to perform successfully

schwa the "empty" vowel in an unaccented syllable, such as the last syllable of *circus* and *bagel*

semantics the study of word and phrase meanings

shallow word learning partial or limited knowledge of a word that may be constricted to one context or one meaning instead of several

sound-symbol correspondence same as phoneme-grapheme correspondence; the rules and patterns by which letters and letter combinations represent speech sounds

structural analysis the study of affixes, base words, and roots

suffix a derivational morpheme added to a root or base that often changes the word's part of speech and that modifies its meaning

syllable the unit of pronunciation that is organized around a vowel, it may or may not have consonants before or after the vowel

syllabic consonants /m/, /n/, /l/, and /r/ can do the job of a vowel and make an unaccented syllable at the ends of words such as rhythm, mitten, little, and letter

syntax the rule system by which words can be ordered in sentences

vocabulary the body of words known by the speaker of a language, receptive or listening vocabulary is the body of word meanings recognized in context, whereas expressive vocabulary is the body of word meanings known well enough that they can be used appropriately by the speaker of a language

vowel one of a set of 15 vowel phonemes in English, not including vowel-r combinations; an open phoneme that is the nucleus of every syllable; classified by tongue position and height (high-low, front-back)

word recognition the instant recognition of a whole word in print